Jenny

One

Two

Three

Sean Walsh

**Single Parent,
Two Wee Attachments –
sorry, Assets!**

Copyright © 2023 by Sean Walsh
All rights reserved. No part of this publication may be reproduced, stored in or introduced into a retrieval system, or transmitted, in any form, or by any means (electronic, mechanical, photocopying, recording, or otherwise) without the prior written permission of the copyright owner or his agent.

Gone Daughter

I climb the stairway to the attic
- 'clear day… dim lit night -
into an empty room full of
Might Have Been…

'Cross to the slanted ceiling,
lever open the window,
look out across slated roofs,
dull-bricked chimneys,
towards Dublin Bay,
the Migrant Way…

CONTENTS

Gone Daughter	2
Dedication	6
I'm Outa Here!	9
Ann? A Word…	41
Runaways	79
Homeland	91
Square Peg One	97
Square Peg Two	98
The Keyboard Kid	106
Victors One, Two	114
The Graduate	118
Home for Christmas	123
Come in, Jenny Three!	134
Catch up	142
Tough love, Dad!	154

First Impressions

'**Once started I could not stop**… It is an amazing piece of work that defies classification.

It is so many things in so many wonderful ways, in so many creative forms, with so many challenging time-shifts, emotional-shifts, narrative shifts - all explored, developed and drawn together in a sweep of literary magic.

The writing is at times poetic, ever beautiful and sensitive; at other times brilliantly dramatic…

It is, at heart, a warm delicate piece - and your pride in the Jennies, and their love for you, is never ever far away from us, the listeners and the watchers.

It will live on, in other times, in other hands. It will be housed, loved and treasured, way beyond its literary brilliance and its deserved literary applause.

Bernard Farrell.

'**Just finished** *Jenny One Two Three* and am, to use your own word, gobsmacked. It's a tour de force, deeply personal…

There is poetry in the writing and the interweaving of different stories, letters, photographs make it a compelling piece for the reader…

A unique piece to say the least, full of heartbreak and triumph… You have achieved a cleansing of sorts, which is, when all is said and done, the reason why we write…

John Liddy.

It is certainly the most absorbing reflection by a father on his relationship with his daughters that I have ever read.

I was deeply impressed by the qualities of truth and love which shine through it from beginning to end. All of the human heart seems to be there.

It is so deeply rooted in the soil of your life. Love is the thread that runs through everything, the agony and ecstasy, the heartbreak and the joyous celebration. It bears out Paul's statement, *'Love never ends'*.

It is often deepened in suffering and struggle. I am sure it would speak to all parents and daughters (and sons).

Your way of expressing all that rich experience is as striking as ever – direct, immediate, finely honed, beautifully crafted.
Thank you for sharing – and yourself…

Martin Hogan.

Dedication

To Joanna and Siobhan – who else?!

*"Your writing is deep, penned with emotion and love
 so comes from your heart to mine…*

*Have you shared with your girls? I think it would be
 wonderful if you do.*

Your love for them… I read, hear… they need to know it!"
 - Anonymous.

Jenny. My mother's name.

I remember her saying to me – *"I was hoping you'd call one of yours after me."* Jolt. Oh, dear. It hadn't occurred to me…

My weens. Siobhan and Joanna. When they started school it turned out they both had the same name – in Irish! 'Didn't even get that right!

Little angels. Charming. As Joan, my late sister-in-law, once put it – *"You'd beg the earth with them…"*

Indeed. Lovely while it lasted. And then? Then? The teenage years! Oh-hh!.. 'Nuff said… So when I came to write about them, they fused in my memory, imagination, became as one. That one I named Jenny.

And when I set out to chart the stages they passed through – infancy, adolescence, girlhood - the title of the script I was working on came to me: *Jenny One, Two, Three…*

Broadcast on RTE One, BBC 4 and, in German, on WDR, Cologne, it struck a chord in the heart of many a listener…
'Made a first impression as a chapter in my magnum opus: *Notes on the Past Imperfect.* (Amazon and Smashwords.)

You'd beg the earth with them…

**And now a further, final morph:
a memoir of sorts, memorabilia…
photos, clippings, comments…
dialogue, monologue…
poetry, prose, reviews…
scrapbook.**

I'm Out a Here!

When she took off I gave her a month,
'month at the most...
She'll be back, I'll take bets on it.
Down at the mouth, sure,
but glad to be home for all that:
safe, secure, shelter…
Oh yeah, London'll cure her cough.

Oh, Jenny, Jenny!..
*What are you at, a tall a tall, daughter mine?..
I didn't give you a hope - how could I?..*

*Sure I knew the time would come
when you'd want to fly the nest. Sure I did.
But I wanted so much you to have
something going for you -
so you wouldn't be going to nothing...*

*Learning the hard way...
skimping on this, going without that,
maybe borrowing, on pay day, your fare to work.*

Answering one small ad after another after an -
hoping against hope for an interview:
a chance to talk, bluff, lie your way
unto the first rung of an endless ladder
getting - nowhere…

But the weeks passed. And the seasons.
She hung in there, held out, roughing it.
No way would she give in. Pride?.. But of course.
And a strong resolve to stand and give challenge.
But kept in touch - the occasional letter,
the seldom phone call.

'Came the day I booked a flight,
packed an overnight, made a phone call,
boarded for Heathrow,
then on to London Central…

I wanted to see my daughter, that's the why!

Jenny! Jenny, over here!
Dad! Oh, it's great to see you, Dad!
Now… let me look at you... Hmmm...

What, Dad - what?..
Well... For one thing, you're too thin in the face
and too much on the hips...
D-a-d!?
You've been eating all the wrong food, I know, I can tell -
Ah, Dad...
For another... I can't take my eyes off you!
Oh, Dad, that is so-oooo! -
Jenny, Jenny Alana!..

We walked and talked -
bumping, laughing, nodding,
skirting, glancing,
taking each other's measure -
until we came to a restaurant on a side street
that looked just the job...

How do you like your spaghetti, kiddo? Al dente?..

To be honest, she was far more interested
in the homemade ice cream smothered
in chocolate sauce!
Still only a child in ways, my Jenny...

Over coffee she fished a camera

from a mighty hold-all -

and a passing waiter duly obliged.

Click!

Just you and me, Dadsers!

And when she excused herself to go to the loo,

I knew she was having a quick drag.

But not in front of her old man.

Not yet. Not quite yet...

'Came the time to finish, settle, tip,

exit into the crisp night air,

the emptying streets... the Underground.

I to my hotel,

she to her burrow in outer suburbia.

Down and down again... cavernous... dim lights...

echoing footsteps... eerie, outer-space noises.

We waited, platforming with the other,

gathering, late-nighters...

Will you be all right, Dad? You know where to change?
Write, won't you? You have no idea how much it -

I stepped into an empty carriage,
turned, and our eyes met:

Oh, but I do, I do... I'll ring you, Jenny. Soon as I -

No! The doors edged shut and it was moving,
gathering sudden speed...

Jenny static, riveted,
eyes brimming, limp hand lifted -
Then she was gone... I was gone.

They opened again at the next station...
In a way, they had closed for good.
And so much gone unsaid.
So much beyond and below the chatter,
chit chat, small talk…
A hundred - oh, a thousand - things
left unspoken, unshared...
I to her, she to me.

I, I left something of myself on that platform.

Behind, on that platform.

And even if I wanted it back?

But I wouldn't - wouldn't ever want it back.

God go with you, Jenny... I can't...

Yes. Yes, that's the way of it... No holding on.

Let her be… chart her own course… into deep water.

Had it framed, the print she sent me.

Not a great photo, not much of a camera.

Still, when I light the fire of a winter's evening,

draw back the curtains, switch on

the occasional lights…

it seems to somehow catch the glow:
Jenny. Jenny Alana and me,
arm in arm in El Corvo –
a chocolate-sauce-over-ice-cream
ristorante…

"A thoroughly beautiful piece,
perfection in writing and the method used.
It was so alive, you involved me the reader
so engagingly… a wonderful experience…
Thank you for sharing."
            Face Booker.

'Remember *www.writing4all.com*?

No? A website for scribblers starting out on The Rocky Road… It was great - while it lasted. Not sure why it gave up, lack of funds maybe? I came upon it quite by chance in the 90's and approached with caution.

I need not have worried. I was given a warm welcome by beginners from Ireland to New Zealand, the Americas to South Africa. All with one thing in common: the pen and how we use it, creatively…

Encouraged by all I read - comments, constructive critique - I soon decided to test the waters. A short piece or two, taken out of the bottom drawer and dusted down. The result was almost instant. Enthusiasm, encouragement...

More, more!.. From faraway Brisbane - and a lady (Barbara?) who came to describe herself as *Your Aussie friend* - to contacts and comments much nearer home...

And it was on this site that samples of my writing first came to be described as Poetry. I kid you not. Poetry! What, me a poet?! I had given up on couplets and similar stuff long since - not for me!

Yet here were fellow scribes assuring me that what I had written was poetry - in free style. Free style? I had never heard of it! But for me it was a new lease of life, the key to wondrous freedom, a license to self expression that lifted a weight off my shoulders...

I began to go back over what I had already written - sifting here, mining there… exploring, discovering, re-working, polishing… giving birth anew.

'Sad that this site folded. 'Sad that I lost all my contacts - I knew them only by their pen names... But for their encouragement I might never have gone on to publish *New Leaf... Pen Pal... Memorare... The McMaster Piece... Wee Nudge* - and so many other 'keepers...'

And when I came to post *I'm Outa Here!* the response of readers blew me away!

__It is a beautiful writ__, Fra Innocente,* so beautiful, you left a bit of me back there on that platform, too.

I have tears in my eyes, I love the two voices within this poem. I love the photo, so wonderful to end it with the photo. You have taken me on a journey through the life of a father and daughter, so precious, your visit to her and her joy at seeing you, you her.

__I thank you__ for sharing this wonderful heart to heart love of your daughter. As a daughter and a mother, it is wonderful to hear the father's view, it was heart rending for me and has made me think about my dad and myself... but we don't talk about such things.

* My pen name as a member of Writing4All.com

I do talk heart to heart to my father, *I have always done so but I am saddened that he will leave this world not really having known me. I left for foreign climes in my 20's. I have done so much in my life that my father did not share or does not know.*

I just might tell him when I visit him in two weeks time for his 81st birthday. Sadly he cannot speak anymore so he will not be able to respond but this poem has made me think about it. Thank you!

I'm keeping this!.. (Face Booker)

The one thing *that came across powerfully to me was your deep love for Jenny and her love for you – it touched me to the core of my being. I love the words you often spoke to her –"Alana…" 'Beautiful.*

I adore my dad, *it is a good idea to tell him. Your poem helped me so much, Sean, thank you. I look forward to reading more of your work, you have such a wonderful style of writing, you are probably a published poet, I will check your profile now. A huge thanks!!*

This is a beautiful *piece of writing. I felt very emotional reading it, especially the end looking at the photo on the mantelpiece, that really struck a chord. We find it very hard to let go of our children. We love them and worry about them, you articulate all these emotions so well in your poem.*

This wee girl, holding my hand,
clinging to me…
wanting – oh, longing! – to be molded.
And I, I paid her scant attention.
Thinking, years and years yet a growing,
plenty of time to, to…
More fool me.

Wee Wet Blue Eyes

Oh, but she was a gorgeous child!
Pig tails flying in the wind,
freckles framing a ha'penny nose,
hop-hop-hop scotching
outside our front window,
safe on a tar macadam road,
secure in a quiet cul-de-sac in snug suburbia...

I eased into second gear, swung round the corner,
pulled up at our semi…
I was getting out, reaching for jacket and brief case,
when she sighted me.

A squeal of delight and she was dashing forward,
eyes dancing, face radiant,
knowing I would turn to meet and greet her,
sweep her up and into my arms, shower her with -

Suddenly she tripped, pitched, sprawled.
A stricken silence –
then the pain, shock, sobbing embarrassment...

Oh, Daddy... Daddy!

I hurried forward... lifted, carried her indoors…
the other kids turning away, awkward,
head-dropping in quiet sympathy…

There, there. Hush, love, hush. Sssshhhh...
Show me. Oh, dear, dear...
Your poor palms and your knee, bleeding...
Come on, now, come on...
Sure, we'll have you right as rain in no time...

I'll sponge away the grit and grime
and there's plasters in the kitchen press
where we keep the cough bottle and the liniment...

No, no it won't hurt.
I would never hurt you,
don't you know that?
No, nor let anyone else hurt you.
My girl, aren't you?..

You got a fright, that's what it is...
Hmmm?.. What's that?.. Tripped?

No, no you didn't trip, Jenny.
No, the road jumped up and hit you,
that's what happened...
Bold. Bold road...

'There now, see?.. You're smiling again...
Yeah! And, and laughing!..

Jenny... My Jenny... Wee wet Blue Eyes...

First Communion

Jenny looking out from 'neath a veil:
open-eyed... trusting... distrusting...
unaware of what was out there,
what lay ahead… in the world beyond
home and hearth and convent school.

All she knew that morning
was that white was for purity, innocence,
that Jesus was coming to her,
really and truly present
in the sacrament of the Altar.

A wafer on her tongue, distilling within her,
Love, Peace, Serenity –
a stillness of mind and body.

How's this it went?..

*"You have given yourself to me,
now let me give myself to Thee...
I give you my heart that it may always love you…"*

'Knew, besides, that later there would be
congratulations, celebrations,
goodies and silver and notes
in her rosary purse…

And by her side, so proud of her,
parents she was justly proud of...
Hairdo, outfit, suit, tie, shoes shining.

*"In a bit closer... look at the camera...
Now smile, big smile... Ah, that's it..."*

Golden day of golden days...
before the storm clouds gathered
and the rancour of marital strife
rent the domestic fabric...

**They were mine, no matter what. And I loved them both the
same... and always will....**

'Seems like yesterday
she was going to bed with her dolls
and the toy horses on her locker
coming to life - large as life -
cantering, ever so gracefully,
round and around her room,
lulling her, in slow motion,
to heavy-lidded sleep...

'Night I walked the floor with her...
there and back, there and back.
Cradling her in my arms... her whimpering,
head on my shoulder.
Unbearable pain... searing ear ache...
Waiting for the doctor on call to arrive,
diagnose, prescribe… depart, fee-paid...

Only the two of us, eh Dad?.. Dadsers.

Not any more. Just me now. Me and the four walls.
Not even the dog for company... Traffic, huh.
How he came by the name, I'll never know...

I didn't tell her. Jenny. Hadn't the heart.
A letter?.. Yes, yes that would be...
how he began to tilt - slowing, going blind...

The Vet and back, the Vet and back…

That last night I stayed up
into the wee small hours,
him shivering, sickening, shaking...
on the bed I had made up in front of the fire...
until he... 'till he... Traffic.

She'll die when she hears...
Oh, but she loved that mongrel.
'Used to talk to him. And he to her.
Sometimes. I think...
Chemistry. Vibes. All that...
'Bit weird, if you ask me.

But then, her mother used to talk to the cat –
before she got fed up waiting for a bite to eat
and fecked off with herself...

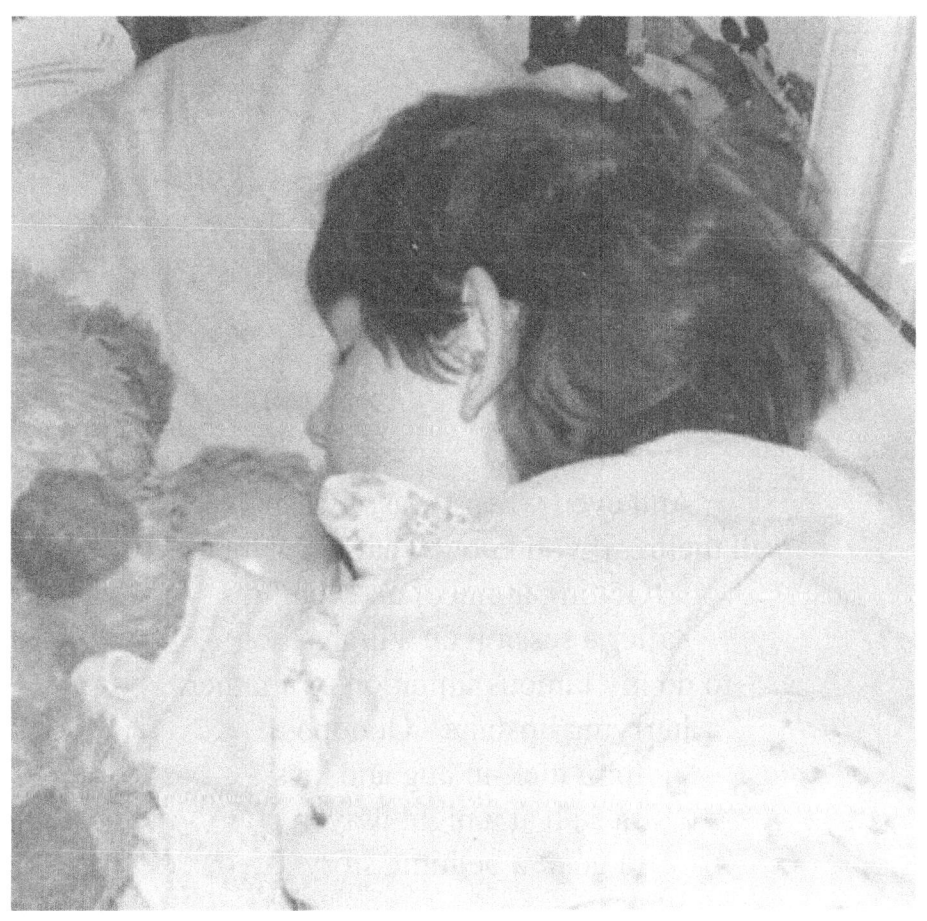

Could you blame her?..
Jenny. 'Talking to the dog.
'Bout the only company she had, betimes.

Well, her mother was forever coming and going:
in one door, out the other...
And sure half the time I was elsewhere –
off chasing a story here, an angle there.
Or pinned down in town,
filing copy for the early edition...

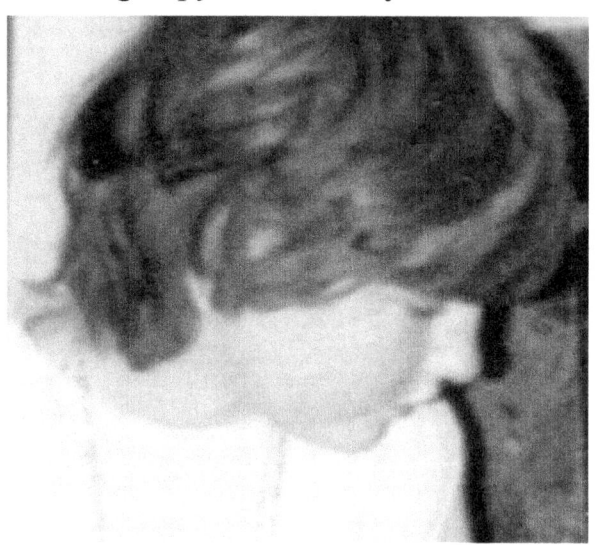

And even when I was, I wasn't –
all there... if you know what I... 'Not all...
'Getting home of an evening
after a session on a high stool
to do my famous imitation of a father:
hurrying upstairs - Ooooppss! –
for a tuck-in hug and kiss,
a stab at a night prayer,
a go at a bedtime story...

Don't forget to say your prayers, Jenny...

'Always... No matter how - how you're feelin'...
Even a, a few words – and mean 'em.
Better'an nothin'...

"As I lay down my head to sleep
I pray to God my soul to keep...
Is he in Heaven or is he in Hell, that damned elusive –"

D-a-a-d?! That's not how it goes!..

Oh?!.. Sorry, love. 'Teaching you the wrong one.
Sorry, God. 'Went off the rails there for a minute.
A bit... 'Get it right. Tomorrow night...
'Make a fresh start... To-tomorrow... 'Nother day...

What?! Tell, tell you a story? Ah-hhh... Look, it's getting late, Jenny, and you have to be –

Well, it'll have to be a quick one – I, I'm very...

"Once... once upon a time... there was an old, old..."

Oh, I did try - now and then, here and there,
to be a, a parent... 'real Dad...
just like the other men in the Estate.

Like, like the day I took her to the pool...

That's it, that's the girl...
Push with your legs...
Hands cupped, under your chin...
Now sweep out, out with your arms...
Push, push with your legs...
Now glide... Easy, nice and...

Yes! That's it! See, you can swim!
Ah, that's my Jenny...
Hmmm?.. 'Deep end?..
Well... all right, then...
Just hold on to me, okay? I won't let you...
Here we go, now... Easy, easy does it...
All right?..

Oooooopps!..
Okay, okay, I have you!..
It's all right, all right, Jenny...
Just a slip, that's all...

No, of course... 'course I won't let go...
I played it down. But yes, yeah...
'No denying… she got a fright.

We stayed with it, though,
stayed in there until
her fear of the deep began to abate...

We went back the following week,
and the following... and the one after that.

But then… then it just seemed to fizzle out.

Me. My fault... 'Didn't get back in time…

or, or there was something else on...

or I, I just lost interest… to be honest.

Honest? Huh. Honest...

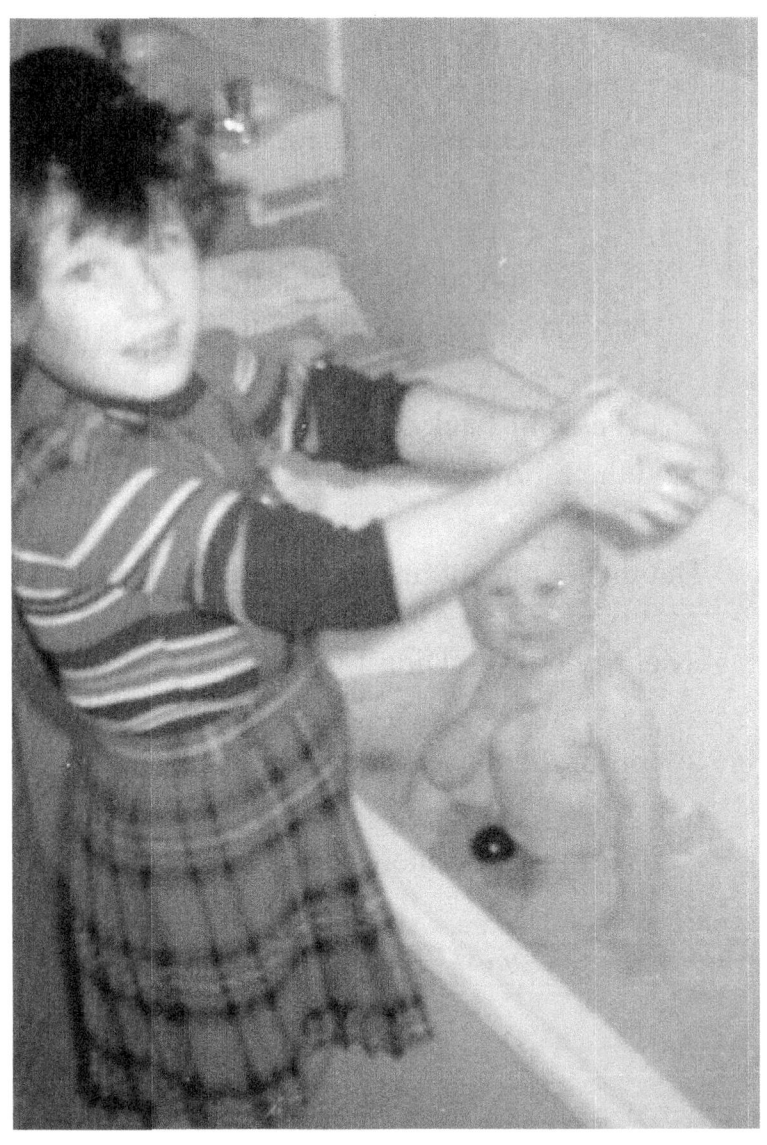

**Jenny One: cast in the role of Little Mother
from an early age…**

'Times Jenny Two drove her mad!

**Most times – most other times –
she was, is, a most precious possession.**

"We wish you a merry Christmas!.. And a happy..."
Did I? Really?.. Wish you a Merry Christmas,
Jenny? You know, like -
Cosy, cuddly, nice-to-be-here,
never-to-be-forgotten?..

Presents and cards and crackers...
Lights on a real tree by the window
in the front room...
And telly, telly!...
Wondrous entertainment in glorious colour!
Y-e-a-a-a-hhh!

*"Lots of chocolate for me to eat,
Lots of coal making lots of heat...
Oh, wouldn't it be..."*

Christmas Eve... I got it right - for once.
The shopping, the fuel, the decorations...
All that day I was the model father –
whatever about an ideal husband...

And no booze. 'Not as much as wet the lips...
Later on - oh, well before the shops shut –
I sallied forth one last time...
'Special, oh a very special assignment:
to buy Jenny's very own present...

Hey, there's my local and look,
look at the cars outside!
Some of my best buddies in there,
the cream of the club...
'Bet the craic is only ninty…

Just the one?.. A quickie?..
Come on, pull over!
Indicate, turn the wheel –
or did it turn by itself?..
One beer, wish them all the best
and you're on your way...

'Still plenty of time to buy
that very special - whatever.
Ease into second... unto a high stool...

"Well, will you look who's here?..

If it isn't himself!..

We were only talking about you this –

Here, come 're - what are ya havin'?"

The first pint went down like velvet,
the second was mother's milk...
and when I stood up to go, car keys in hand,
someone had sent me over a short,
compliments of the Season...

I slumped... feet nailed to the floor...
Cru-crucified...
Gluepot... Bloody gluepot!
I was still there coming up to closing...

Frost on the ground... 'windscreen.
Put her on pilot... Slow home.
Ease in the door... Schhhhh...
Not a sound... Them asleep above...
Empty... empty-handed.

She'd wake in the morning –
"Hurray! It's Christmas!" –

and hurry downstairs in nightie
and slippers and dressing gown
and high excitement -
to the lounge,
the Christmas tree and –
nothing...

'Nothing but the heavy snoring
from the master bedroom en-suite.

Oh, you cripple! You contemptible Self!..

Incredibly, she forgave me... in time.
Oh, yes... indeed.

'Only remains for me to, to forgive myself.

Maybe... some day...

Storm Trooper

Ah, years ago, now.
I checked into an inner city hospital:
gaunt, red-bricked, Victorian.
'Creaking all the way from
Main Entrance to X Ray,
Reception to Theatre,
Canteen to Cardiology...

A Men's Ward that seemed to stretch forever
across a sea of russet linoleum
to Dickensian lavatories.
Floor polish and disinfectant,
Harassed nurses, whirling past,
fighting fatigue, resolute in white.

The old and the old-before-their-time:
empty-eyed, withdrawn, distressed.

Smokers coughing abominable sputum.

The camaraderie of an optimistic few:
wheezing gems of wisdom –
honed bons mots –
in pristine Dublinese.

And then it happened.

The January of the Deep Freeze:
storm winds beating against the windows,
snow swirling down, blanketing,
from an ink sky...

Next day, stand-still:
impassable roads, treacherous pavements…

"You wouldn't put out a milk bottle…"

Yet she made it. Jenny. In to see me.
Lurching, slipping, swaying, falling...
'Determined to reach me on the eve
of the Big Knife.

I glanced up from a so-so weekly
to find her at the end of my bed:
smiling, glowing, radiant,
melting snow on anorak and headgear,
exuberant at the challenge of it all.

Jenny?... But how - ? No, I mean...
Oh-hh… Ah, come 'ere to me...
Jenny… Jenny Alana!

Now… here's a thing… When I first put this piece "out there" it was longer than above. Like so:

Oh, Dad! Dad, will you be all right? God, Dad, if anything happened to you I, I don't know what I'd... I'd be lost. No, Dad you're to come home to us, safe and well, have to!

Mum sends all her love, she'll be in to see you soon as - She'll ring in the morning, first thing, to find out how - how... Dad, I'm using all your tissues...

Lovely. I was content enough. Until the following arrived from Down Under:

"It's a fine piece, Fra Innocente, deep with honest emotions. And I really felt like I was there in that hospital with you, all the way.

The lines flow effortlessly right through and up to your daughter's arrival... the joy of that, her overcoming of that foul weather, your young storm trooper indeed..

But here I go again...I would cut it there after you have spoken to her. It feels right to me that she does not speak. Her presence now says it all, is enough, is more than enough... So silence now, time for the close-up, the emotions complex on her loving face... No dialogue needed, no more words!!!

I wouldn't change a syllable prior to that... because all the lines are marvelous... But that final cut - I do suggest it? What do you think? Just my opinion of course..

Your Aussie mate…

BARBARA XX."

(Her name on **Writing4All.com**, mine was Fra Innocente; a pen name was a condition of membership. I think she lived in Brisbane, but I'm not sure.)

Dilemma, indeed. Sean on the rack… What to do, what to do?.. even as these golden words of Quiller Couch came to mind: *You must learn to murder your darlings…*

(Q C to his friends. The Art of Writing by Sir Arthur Quiller Couch. Some copies "out there." Go google…)

'Mulling over Mark 1… Mark 2… aware it was up to me to call it… I printed out both versions, placed them side by side on my desk…

And though friends and well-wishers, privately circulated, cautioned against deleting Jenny's monologue, I took a deep breath and quietly, in the final analysis, did just that.

Photo finish! Down Under, thumbs up!

Thank you, Lady Barbara…

Aside…

Ann?.. A word…

*What's all this I'm hearing
about you and your latest?!
'You can't be serious?.. What?!*

'Take up with the likes o' your man?..

Are you gone soft in the head or what?

Is there a full moon?!

'Know what you'd be letting yourself in for?

*A smoker, drinker – and I don't mean casual,
I'm talking chronic, addictive.
'Panics if he hasn't a fag…
Every night, nearly, off to his local
for the last hour… topping up.*

And you're thinking of hitching up with him?!

*'Wife walked out leaving him with two childer -
and from what I hear they'll be gone wild altogether
before not too much longer…*

*Can you not see? You'd be dropping into his lap
if you took it on yourself to mother them!..*

*And he'd be ever so grateful – oh, wouldn't he, just!
'Thanking his lucky stars – and God, if he has a god -
telling his boozing pals it's all his birthdays in one!*

Your own family, *Ann –*
have you given them a thought?
'Your father and mother still alive,
good living, respectable people.
What are they going to think?
What'll they say?..
"He saw you coming!"
And they'd be right!

His weens, *have you met them?..*
They, they ran to you?.. I see.
'Had them primed beforehand,
two trump cards.

There's no doubt in my mind, Ann –
he's way ahead of you…
Oh sure, lovely. Wee innocents.
But growing all the while…
'Teenagers before you'd know it.
And after that? 'You think
they're going to hang about? Eh-hh?
After what they've been through?

You're not serious? What! The - the Arts?
'That how he makes a living?.. Ah, Holy God!
And me thinking it couldn't get any worse...
As me poor father would say, God rest him,
"The arts me arse, commerce is your man!"

Just think for a minute, will you?
Prospects?.. Promotion?.. Pension?..
Well?.. Dicey, eh? Should I be surprised?..

You told him about your own job,
I suppose?
So he knows he can always
fall back on you if all comes to all…

He's a cuckoo, Ann –

and he has his eye on your nest!..

Smile? Is that all you can - ? Oh, no!?.
'That what's going through your head?
'Once you have him, you'll change him...'
'You're not – surely not – that foolish?!
Change him? HIM?!

'You think he'll put the cork back in the bottle –
stub out his last smoke –
because you disapprove... tut tut tut?..
'Stay in, stop going out at night,
say so long to the lads?..

Ha!.. What a hope you have…

Ann?.. Are you listening to a word I?-

Ah-hh... Good night...

Yet she did – against all the odds…
Sean beginning – at least beginning –
to pick up fragments
from a shattered mirror…

Slowly coming to realise:
alcohol and Creativity
make strange bedfellows…

'Took a while, mind...
No miracles, no instant cures.

Patience. Perseverance. Prayer.
Oh, yes – Prayer!

Amazing grace... Ann.
'Saving her man from himself –
and giving their Dad back
to two girls a growing…

Our first home in the city, Dublin 7.

Some nest – some cuckoo…

Jenny?..

Try. Again?.. Again…

Reach out to her.

Only this time, follow through,

make it stick…

***Jenny?.. Jenny, how about** you and me
going to Mass on Sunday? The eleven, say…
Are you game? Have we a date?
How do you mean – cool?..*

So... At week's end I will clean the slate,
descend on some unfortunate priest.
Ha. He won't know what hit him!
And if he's nodding off when I step in, well...

Back row, centre aisle.

A tangible stillness in a dim-lit Church:

elders moving slowly -

genuflecting, kneeling, standing -

making their way to Calvary,

treading their very own,

plaster statued, Via Dolorosa.

Re-living the Greatest Story Ever Told

in reparation for their own sins

and the sins of the whole world..

Jesus is condemned... the weeping women...
Falls the second time... Veil of Veronica...
Nailed to the Cross... 'Company of thieves...
Sitio, I thirst... Sponge of vinegar...

Stopping, betimes, to nod, whisper, chin-chin -
in-house salutations, parochial palaver -
silhouetted against flickering candles,
framed by altar lights,
passing by the stray soul nursing
a lukewarm radiator…

Pausing to petition the Sacred Heart,
Our Lady of the Miraculous Medal,
Saint Anthony, the Little Flower:
'grace of final perseverance,
'grace of a happy death...
and so to the Beatific Vision.

Clink clank of copper and silver
into Offerings Box:
for the maintenance of the Sanctuary...

the new roof... the Foreign Missions...

the poor that are always with us…

But where the crowds, the queues,

the thronging congregations of Yesteryear?

Singing out with one voice a hymn to Mary?

Whatever happened to Saturday night?..

Red glow over drawn curtains

of Confessional:

invitation to reconciliation...

Should I..? Will I?..

Ah, do. Do in the name o' God.

Open the door, step in, kneel by

a walled Crucifix,

whisper through a grill, darkly,

when the slide's drawn back...

Yes, but how am I going to tell him all?

And will he shoot me down, bawl me out?..

'In this day and age? Hardly...

Bless me, Father, for I have sinned...
It's a while now since my last...
Well, I stayed away because...
I, I'm married, Father, and then again,
I'm not - if, if you know what I...
She, she went away... 'Someone else...

Since then I, I've had a go at the Commandments.
Yes, you could say that: some more than others...

Eh, just the one. She'll be ten in another wee while...
Oh, no, she's with me - except the odd weekend...
Ah, the best I can... 'Not easy.

To be honest with you, I'm not much of a parent,
even at the best of times.
And at the worst I, I can be a holy terror.

Well, like, coming the heavy... Or letting her down...
Raising my voice - maybe even giving the odd roar –
when things don't go to my liking.
Or I, I'm a bit under the weather...
It's that more than anything..

I mean, if there's a sin at all on my soul
I'd like lifted,
it's the way I go on at times
with my young one...

So I, I'd just like to make the peace with Himself...
I will, Father. I'll try again...

He gave me the Rosary. The Sorrowful Mysteries. 'Commended me to Our Lady. I'm never to forget that Salvation came to us through a woman... Ha.

Sorry. 'Sorry, Lord. I, I'll try... Again? Again...
Getting up, falling down...
The Agony in the... 'Dark in Gethsemani.
Or was there a full moon?
Between ominous clouds, gathering...

Forgive us our trespasses... as we forgive those...

As I, I for... forgive... her. Wife.
There, I've said it. And I'll try –
try the best I can - to, to mean it...

Turn the other cheek, eh?
Take it, full force, in the face, to the jaw.
Tilt. Incline head in submissive anticipation
of another shock to the system...

Not seven times but seventy times seven...

There y'are. That's Christianity for you.
Difficult? It's just about bloody well impossible!

Lead us not into… deliver us from...

Deliver me, Lord.
Please deliver me from –
me, myself.
Free me from this,
this wallowing in the past.
Spare me the torture
of riveting recall...

Memorare

Hail Mary... Hi... Hello?
Are you there - or are you on your travels?
Above - or beyond in Yugoslavia?

I, I'm never too sure when I have you,
to be honest. But then, you're a female.
So I don't find it all that surprising...

My mother *was always there and me growing up.*
When I got home from school or in off the streets
or back from the pictures or after a football match
or, or if I was in a fight with some other gang,
she was there. 'Always seemed to be - there.
'Can't remember a time she wasn't...

There was this shrine, as I recall.
Oh, well known it was, locally...
We walked the three miles, there and back.
'Out the country, 'summer's day…
Six miles in all. A killer…

'Knelt for the Rosary. Nudging, gawking around,
stifling a giggle... Every bead a penance...
'Grass trodden underfoot by previous pilgrims.

The tree and the hollow, the rock and the glade,
the stream where we filled our bottles to carry home.
Our salute to you wafting out on the warm, still air:

'Calling to pray... Ave... Ave... Ave Maria...

The Lourdes statue marking the ledge
where you appeared... whenever it was,
to whoever it was... reputedly.

We had you to ourselves in those days -
before you took off on a world tour...

Holy Mary, Mother of God...

And mine. My mother... Yes? Hmmm...
Well, I'll tell you, straight up:
they're not all like you. Women.
Some of them can be right - !
Ah, I won't say it out – out of respect...

You... you came through it all
with hardly a scratch, so they tell me.
And now you're on a direct line to Himself:
easy access, unlimited credit,
excellent equity, buoyant stock –
in-in-interceding for us...

All I'm asking is that you put in
a good word for me -
hoping you'll understand, even if He doesn't -
so when the time comes
I won't be caught on the wrong foot...

And look, I know you're inundated
with all sorts of prayers and petitions.
But I'd ask you - as a special favour -
to look out for my wee one.

She's heading for the rapids and there's
damn all I can do about it...
Well, you only have to go as far as
the porch if you don't believe me!

Out there in the street: teenagers
on their way to the Pub, Party, Disco, Rave –
paying scant attention to this
granite structure, dim-lit Presbytery...

And in no time at all my wee one
will be one of them:
keeping up, matching their form,
cool, laid-back, with-it,
in thrall to her peer group.
Maybe even a leader?..

So please, will you keep an eye on my Jenny?
God knows, she could do with a bit of mothering.
And why not? Ah, now! 'No better woman...

Do. Oh, please.
Put your mantle about my daughter
and protect - save her.

Oh, I know, there's the nuns and they're doing
their best, I dare say.
But they seem to have their hands full
and they stream, unmercifully,
and if you don't mind me saying so,
their idea of Instruction, Christian Doctrine,
is a far cry from the Penny Catechism...

'Years ago, my wee one,
holding my hand, looking up at me:

'Only the two of us, Dadsers!..

Sure, we're both a bit lost, Jenny,
in our different ways...

Oh, oh. Sacristan swishing down the aisle,
keys ajangle, signalling close-down...
'poised to see off the last of the faithful few.

'Return to house, flat, home, family,
to another, to others, to no one..
The tea or the cocoa, the fire and the hearth,
sober survival...
Multi-channel viewing,
wide choice of alternative worlds…

Dear Jesus, I'm hopeless!
'Can't even say Hi to Your Mum
without going off the rails...

I thought, maybe, Jenny and me
going to Mass together would bring us closer,
help her – me – to stay on the right track,
stick to the straight and narrow...

Ah, but it didn't last.
As she grew older there was the pull
of her peer group,
strong as the swell of the sea...

Our Gang: Jenny centre stage…

One minute she was at my side, the next she was –

Up, Up and Away –

to puberty,

adolescence,

the teenage years

and oh, what divilment!

Sure I knew it was on the way, but still...
Just, it seemed, as I was beginning
to get the hang of Jenny One,
she disappeared, almost without trace.

Enter from far right, Jenny Two.
My offspring had changed –
quietly, irrevocably, almost surreptitiously...
And I, sad to say, changed towards her.

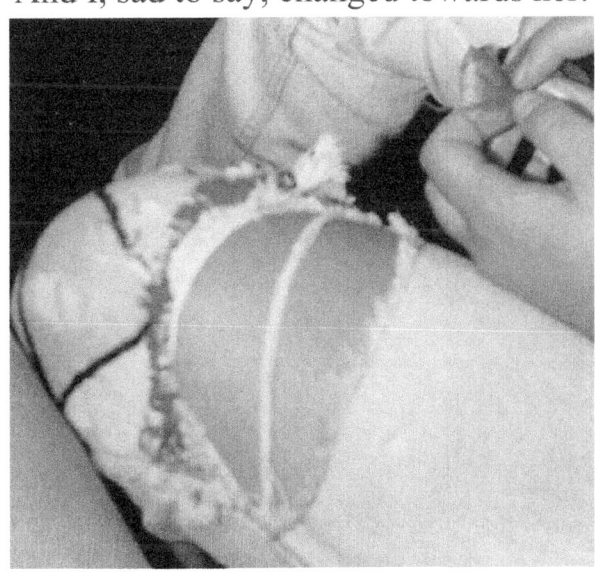

Will you have some of this?..
Huh... 'Not hungry...
Sure how could you be hungry?
'Always stuffin' yourself.

Sweets and biscuits, chocolate and crisps,
gung and gunge...
and you're a hoor for hula hoops...
Is it any wonder you have pimples?..

*And you'll look marvellous with a brace –
oh, a sight for sore eyes!..
'Tired talking to you...
But you won't listen, will you?..
The next thing I know you'll be on the fags.
And then it'll be the hard stuff...
And if you go at that the way you let back
orange and coke,
you'll be hooked in no time...*

*All that Gothic stuff... Black. 'Face like putty.
That thing in her nose... and a pair of boots
the farmers threw out years ago...
Ah-hh... Let her off... let her off!*

Lipstick and eye-liner and perfume,
rings and bangles and jewellery,
men's shirts, waistcoats, pyjamas...
Fellas and dates and discos,
posters and mirrors and blow-driers...
Endless phone calls, ages in the bathroom,
beguiling manipulation,
terrible, terrible tantrums,
and a deafening sound from the stereo...

*"God, give me patience!..
Help me to hold myself together
is all I ask, Sweet Jesus!.."*

How many times –
dear God, how many times! –
did I ask her to pick things up...
not to stuff drawers... cram presses?..
How? How many times?..

Larger-than-life posters spanning a sloping ceiling:

David Bowie... Guns 'n' Roses...

Prints, photos, post cards, snap shots...
glaring graffiti... cartoons of doubtful pedigree.

Blue tack and cello tape, paste and glue,
clips and nails and drawing pins...
Markers and crayons and chalk...
Mounds of dust and fluff atop the wardrobe...

Cigarette papers, spent matches, in a tin under the bed.
Mascara on the duvet, lipstick on the pillow case...
A wasted stylus in the damaged arm
of the record player...

Wads of chewing gum under the student desk.
A lifeless bulb in the reading lamp
meant to help her focus on –
STUDY!

Y'know, I believed her - oh, for ages! –
when she told me this, witnessed to that...

'Took a long time for the penny to drop.

And then it was quite by chance...
when I stumbled across,
checked out, came upon
an incontestable scenario to the contrary...

Only then it began to dawn on me:

my darling daughter was a
seasoned, addictive, compulsive
purveyor of blatant fictions...

'Liar! 'Bloody liar!..'

But when I confronted her she reared up,
bluffed, brazened, swore black and blue,
pitching her voice against mine,
higher and higher still...
Lie upon lousy lie.

'Sank further and further still into a quagmire
of irrelevant protestations, non sequiturs,
a morass of pretentious,
preposterous bullshit!

And a thief into the bargain!

Took, snitched, lifted,
helped herself to anything that took her fancy
without as much as by your leave
or would it be all right if..?

My socks... cigarettes... deodorant...
books... tennis racket... videos...
the loose change on the mantelpiece.

The dinner jacket I seldom wear
and didn't miss for ages –

smuggled out and given, 'on loan,'
to a girl friend from down the way...
Was anything sacrosanct?..

'Made her way through the house
from top to bottom,
examined the contents of every drawer...

'Knew every crook and cranny...
'Could identify - and step over –
every creaking floor board…
slipping out, sneaking back in...

Only after I had faced her
with undeniable evidence, irrefutable proof –
and only after she had simmered down,
cooled off, re-grouped –
did she finally admit to me,
here, here at the top of the stairs –
a sort of confessional
under the skylight -
that yes, she had, had indeed...

Tears and sobbing voice, whispering admission…

Oh-hh-hh... Knife edge at my heart.

What to say?.. What to do?..

I fear for you, girl, I really do...
If you go away from here
to live and work among strangers,
get caught out in a lie,
caught with your hand in the till...
there'll be no absolution,
paternal admonition,
on the carpeted stairs by the banisters...
You'll be on your own...
alone...

Jenny Younger.

Ann... urgent:

- That was Madge on the phone –
- Is she ever off it?
- 'Coming back from town, she spotted Jenny –
- What?
- In O'Connell street. Her and another girl... They, they were chatting with, with...
- Who?
- Two – two sailors.
- Nonsense!
- Madge swears it! 'Felt she had to ring – they were... were –
- Huh?
- Foreign. Off a ship in the –
- Look, let me – Jenny left to go to evening Mass. And then she was to call round to Greta – 'do their homework together –
- I'm with Madge on this, Sean. She is certain it was Jenny she saw, didn't know who the other girl was. It – it could be dangerous.

- So?
- I'd go if I could but I have this meeting I can't -
- Huh. And when I get there – what? They could be anywhere!
- Try, at least try. Go in and look around. It may be nothing, harmless enough. But it could be - !.. You'll never forgive yourself if you, if you... don't...

(TO FEET, RELUCTANTLY)

You'll need your mac, it's beginning to...

I parked on a side street, eased out into a rainy night... 'Walked a short distance, turned a corner into O'Connell street: Cleary's clock to my left... the GPO across from me, the Gresham a distance to my right – and the Savoy cinema...

Nearer the target, I sheltered in a doorway. The nine-to-fivers long since departed, gone their several ways to house, flat, bedsit.
Traffic flowing, the city centre emptying.

And no sign of Jenny, no hint, indicator. I was wet, cold, disgruntled – where is she?!

Then cinema-goers began to emerge - crowds of them –and there they were: white uniforms...excited, carefree girls... I watched, dry mouthed, as Jenny and Sailor Boy hugged and kissed, then parted – '*bye, see you, thanks a mil*' –

'Watched as my daughter and Greta waved farewell, then set off for a bus stop and home... I turned away, hurried back to my car, determined to get there ahead of my
errant daughter…

I was seated in my favourite chair, thumbing an evening tabloid when the front door opened and closed. On sudden impulse – don't ask me why, how – I began to sing a la Gene Kelly:

> "*I'm singing in the rain, just singing in the rain...*"

ENTER JENNY

> "*What a wonderful feeling I'm having again...*"

I BROKE OFF AS SHE CLOSED THE DOOR.

- *Ah, Jenny... You look flushed, have you been running?*
- *No, I –*
- *Maybe it's the reading lamp... So how was it?*
- *What?*
- *Mass.*

- *Oh, eh… The usual.*
- *Grown-ups, mostly, I suppose… Very few young ones.*
- *This is it.*
- *'Wouldn't be the same if you weren't there – you and Greta…*

SHE CROSSED TO THE FRUIT BOWL, SELECTED AN APPLE… SAT.

- *So… who was the celebrant?*
- *What?*
- *Who said the Mass?*
- *Oh, eh… Fa-Father O'Connor.*
- *Father O'Connor? 'On a Wednesday? But that's his day off!.. No, you're way out there, Jenny…*

JENNY LIFTED THE APPLE TO HER MOUTH.

- I know for a fact he's sitting in the back row of the Savoy -

AS SHE BIT I DELIVERED THE K O

this very minute… between two… Spanish… sailors.

JENNY COUGHED, CHOKED, SPLUTTERED…
STOOD UP, TURNED TO LEAVE…
PAUSED AT THE DOOR, FLUSTERED.

- *Italian…*

A WHILE LATER – FRONT DOOR –
ANN HURRIES DOWN THE HALL
AND INTO THE ARENA…

- *I didn't wait for the afters…*
- *You missed all the drama –*
- *Jenny? Is she all right? Did you find her? How is she?*
- *Woo! Woo! Take it easy…*
- *You weren't rough with her?*
- *Not a bit. 'Took more out of me than it did her–*
- *I'll go up to her.*
- *I'd say she's lying on her bed this minute cursing me, her luck…*
- *Ah, God love her.*
- *Wondering how her Dad came by the gift of bi-location…*
- *So tell me all…*

AND I DID. SHE LISTENED INTENTLY,
THEN BEGAN TO MUSE…

- *So… you sheltered in a doorway… not wanting to be seen…*
- *Right.*
- *Collar pulled up around your ears… cap pulled down over your forehead… But no dark glasses?*
- *What are you getting at?*
- *People passing. Didn't they notice you?*
- *Some, yes.*

- And?.. I bet they looked, then looked away… hurried on…
- Well, yes… I suppose… I was looking out for Jenny –

SHE BEGAN TO CHUCKLE…
I FROWNED AT FIRST, THEN JOINED IN AS THE LIGHTER SIDE BEGAN TO DAWN ON ME:

*Loitering with intent…citizen's arrest…
hurried away in a squad car
while Pedro de Lad and our precious bundle
continued to cuddle!?!*

JENNY, OVERHEAD, WONDERING
FOR HOW LONG
WOULD SHE BE GROUNDED?..

SUDDENLY AWARE OF THE LAUGHTER
FROM DOWNSTAIRS:

So what's funny? Screw loose or what?!

'Light, maybe, at the end of the tunnel?..

Jenny Elder.

- *Mister Walsh?*
- *Yes, eh –*
- *Sister Consolata here –*
- *Oh-hh…*
- *I'm afraid Jenny has gone too far this time -*
- *What?*
- *She took another girl's bicycle without permission… rode out through the main gates and didn't come back again for over an hour. 'Bad enough that she's disruptive in class without –*
- *Oh, dear. And me hoping the retreat would -*
- *What?*
- *For her class. The weekend, back here on Sunday night… 'Never saw her so -*
- *Mister Walsh…   PAUSE   There was no retreat.*
- *Oh, no!?*
- *Not in the college. Not for any class…*
- *I – I don't know what to –*
- *I do… I am suspending your daughter for a week. She may return on Monday next but not before.*
- *Well, I –*

- *I regret so doing, Mister Walsh, but feel I have no option. For the good of all the girls in my charge… Good day to you.*

I cradled the receiver and stood
for a frozen forever…

What to do? How to cope?
Confrontation? Anger? Voices raised?..
No. No, not this time. Oh, well beyond anger:
quiet words, deflated voice, stricken…

And when alone, ego in the dock:
doubts, denials, self accusations,
transfer of guilt…

Ann at work, long hours, demanding.
Dad ditto, to the other side of the river.
Jenny grounded, under orders:

Study, girl… Cram. Catch up.
Your only hope… Or you'll be left behind…

And even as I eased away in second
to wedge into the rush hour traffic
I sensed she had other ideas –
and damn all I could do about it!

Coffee… cigs… 'phone…
shower… hair dryer.
TV, video… central heating…
Kitchen… Fridge…
Binge eating.
Compulsive nibbling…

Any suggestions… dear Sister… Consolata?

Runaways.

As time passed - months, seasons - they became more and more restless, urgent to get away, put distance between themselves and home… *"Only way we can be sure we won't get caught…"*

The far off hills, eh? Greener than ever! The good life, a warmer clime, a cheaper way of keeping body and soul together - or so they had been assured by a backpacker recently home from walk-about…

But as the weeks passed and the news from abroad was scarce, thin, seldom, Ann became more and more anxious about their welfare, safety.

__Sorry?..__ Am I hearing you?
You – you want us to fly out there?
To, to try and talk some sense into them?..
May - maybe even get them to, to come home?..
'Back with us?..
Ann, are you losing it altogether
or what's got into you?..
Have you done the sums?
Any idea how much it would put us back?
Flights, hotels, eating out?..

Oh, we've been down this road before –
haven't we just!
What about Junior, eh?
'All the way to Galway to find she was
down in Limerick –
or waitressing in Bally de Hump
when she should have been studying
in that college...

And what had we to show for it
when we got back to base?
An empty tank, a slow puncture and
feck-all sign of a Change of Heart!..

The weekend *we went off for a break,*
leaving her in charge... What about that, then?
Butter wouldn't melt in her mouth
and her promising she'd lock up,
share with Ciara in Larsons
until we got back?
Sure we were hardly gone –
treading Friday afternoon traffic –

when she was on the phone,
ringing round, spreading the word:
Jenny's got a free gaffe…

'Back that Sunday evening.
Return to home, hearth – oh, no?!
Jenny in her room at the
top of the stairs –
dreading the Yale key turning…
the front door… opening, closing.
The deafening silence as we stood
in the hall, the penny dropping…

The hurt, disappointment, let-down…
The creepy-crawly sensation of intruders
'been and gone:
from kitchen to bathroom,
fridge to attic…
Stale cigarette smoke…
empty bottles… broken glass.

And worse by far – broken promises.

Anger, then. Rising to rage.
In my voice as I called up the stairway:
Jenny! Come down here this minute!
Then quietly, Ann at my elbow:

She's only... Too young to –
We were wrong to go off and leave her.
We're to blame – 'still only a...

Sean checking... reducing to simmer.
'Not the first time this lady at my side
had come between Dad and daughter...

All right, all right*... Okay...*
But that was then, this is now – and
now is a whole new ball game!
We didn't push them – far from it.
They wanted out and nothing
would do them but -

So okay*. They're down there now –*
cheap fags so they can smoke their heads off.
And God only knows what else they're up to...

No! No, no, no!.. Save your breath.
This time – for once –
I'm not giving in.
You might as well be talking to the wall
as trying to persuade me!..

That's it, Ann. End of story.
So just forget it! Right?!

NEXT DAY... WHEN THE DUST HAD SETTLED,
DAD MADE A PHONE CALL,
WATCHED BY A VERY DETERMINED WIFE:

"Hello?.. I want to book two seats...
Return...
Dublin Barcelona..."

***They're coming, Sis!** Flights booked and all!*

They haven't checked in anywhere
so we'll have that sorted
when we meet them at the airport.
Thrilled, I am – 'best news ever!..
You… you're very quiet there?..

A welcoming party – and on time!
Both on a high - chattering, smoking, gesticulating…
By train across the city and along the coast
to Sant Pol de Mar and Calella…

And then we saw it: their 'apartment.' Oh-hhh…

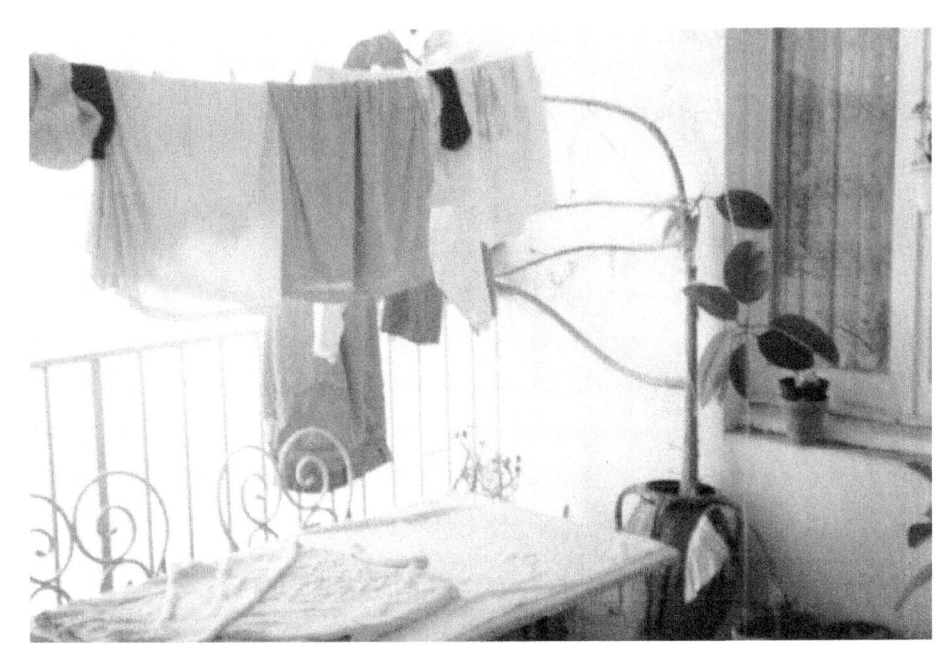

And their work place?
A Brit pub catering for Brit tourists,
our girls out among them, touting…
Or else back at base, out of the sun,
a menu of videos, nicotine, ash trays, coke.

Would boys be less trouble, I wonder?..

Sun, sea – and common sense…
*"It's no life, Jenny…no future.
You're in a cul-de-sac – time to turn back –
back to your own country,
make a life for yourself…"*

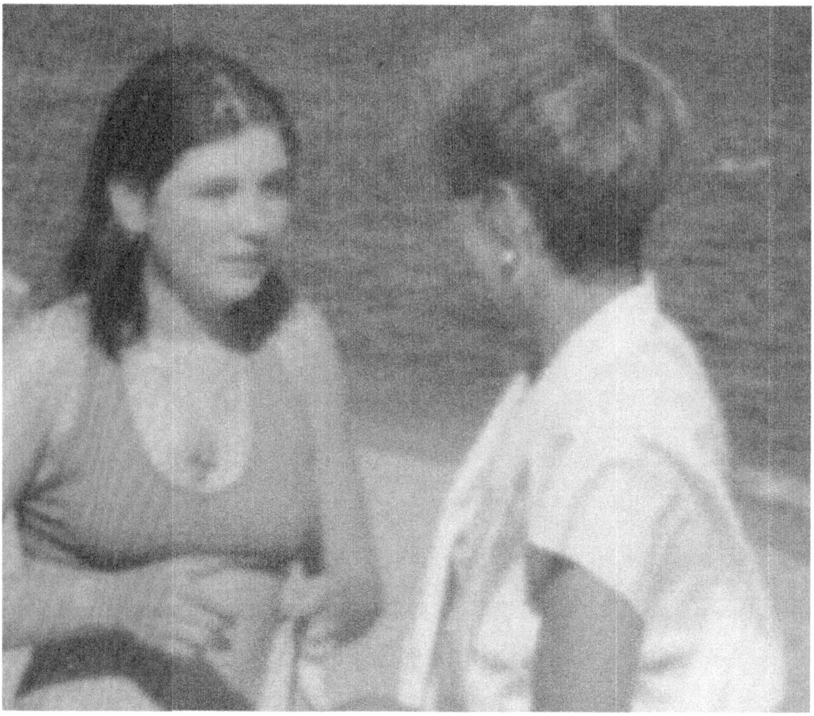

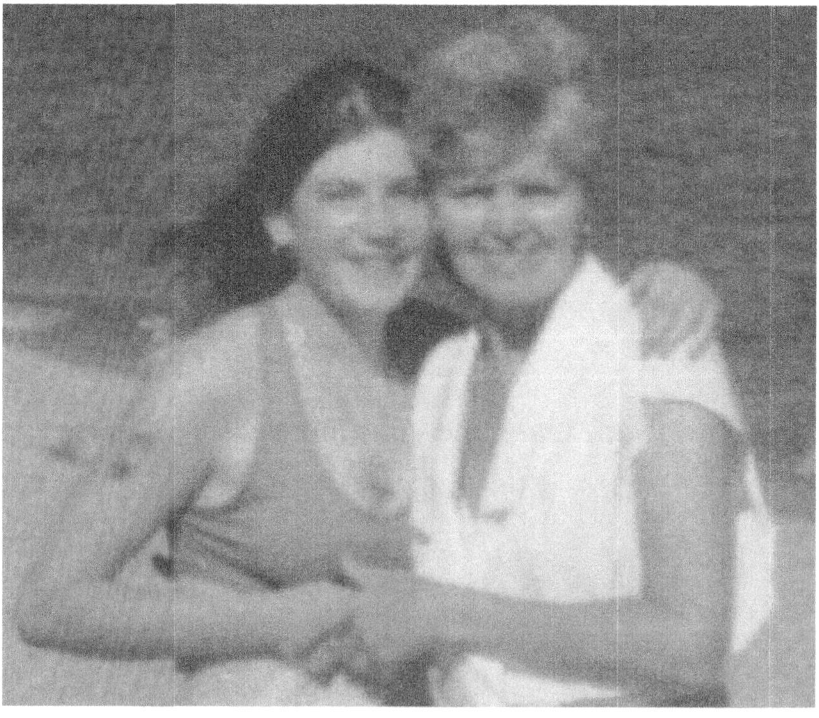

Las Ramblas was something else!
An endless line of shops, cafes, bars, restaurants,
caged birds, floral displays…
A brilliant violinist
backed by a throbbing orchestra…
Row upon row of vendors,
noisy locals, incessant smokers…
'Finishing line at the harbour.

Another day to Montserrat –
by vertical bus!

Up, up and up again!
Don't look out, Ann! Beware vertigo!..

German tourists, unperturbed by the grinding engine,
the wheels dangerously near the edge of the narrow,
broken road winding ever upwards…
listening quietly to the know-all guide
who threw the occasional morsel of English
to the couple from Ireland at the back…

And so to the Benedictine monastery
and the shrine of the black Madonna –
the core and essence of Montserrat.

Ave Maria! Please guard and protect
our wayward daughters.
They're thinking they've arrived –
'still at sea.

And if the tour guide had explained en route
how Ignatius Loyola, founder of the Jesuits,
came to visit, pray, confess, make notes here –
followed by a further sojourn
at out-of-the-way Manresa –
alas, it went right over our heads!

They took it in turn to visit as we took the sun –
and sea – but a stone's throw from our B and B.
Jenny Elder one day, Jenny Younger the next...

And there was the day neither came calling –
over-worked, over-slept after a later than late night?
We waited... and waited... (before mobiles)

Then came our last day,
departure on the morrow.

An early rise, dash to the station,
by train direct to the airport and Check In…

And so much left unsaid, shared –
they to us, we to them.

Will there ever be soul talk, I wondered,
as we crossed Barcelona a final time?..

Homeland

A fair wind and gentle rain greeted us as we stepped from the Aer Lingus jet – ah, the relief! Soon back to a quiet house, the kettle, favourite tea… And as we settled, began to unpack, I fought back the temptation to say – "*I told you so…*"

And yet, and yet… A seed or two had fallen on good soil. Several weeks – and any number of phone calls later - the news from Catalonia was good: the youngest on the phone, joyous, cartwheels… the elder not so much, still hesitant, foot dragging, reluctant to return to the fold…

Did we sub their fares, buy their tickets? To be honest, I can't remember. Nor how they made it in from the airport… But I do recall their arrival in the hall: jumpers and jeans, cartons of duty-free, bundles of washing…

Ann, open-armed. welcoming as ever...

Ah, it's great to be home, Dad!

Ann! Lovely as ever!

A few grey hairs, I'm afraid...

Leave your gear there –

come on down to the Den...

The Comeback Kids

Old Habits die hard.

Sleep…shower, hair wash, blow-dry… Coffee.
Then the video in the front room…
munchies, fags, clouds of smoke...
escape yet again into the Never Never world
of Make Believe, FancyThis, More of That…

And my heart began to sink as I came to realise they had brought their *status quo* with them: waitressing… sleep all morning, wait at table half the night… a free meal and tips, tips… money for munchies, cigs, makeup, a bottle by the neck…
And sadly, never stopping to think they were missing out on - Summer…

As the weeks passed unease set in: edginess, restlessness, impatience, the urge to move on, out, explore yet again, see "what's out there" one last time. 'Away from Dad leaning on them, Ann's quiet routine… (*'My way is best'*)

Sad. And sadder still when the move was not to New York or Berlin, Croatia or Melbourne – but to a few streets away from the family home, to house-sharing with fellow rebels they had met up with along the way - downhill.

Ash tray?.. *'Must be one somewhere - the ad said fully furnished…Use a saucer for now. Or a mug… Tissues?. There's half a toilet roll in the…*

A disco on their night off… Or stay in on *'Broke Nights'* - rent a video, ring the Pizza place, chip in, scramble the price before the delivery guy pulls up at 99 No Hopeville.

End of the month, rent looming… Bum a few bob here, a fiver there...

'Get it back to you as soon as… Ah, you're a brick, Hal!'

    Oh, Jenny, Jenny…
   What are ye at, at all, at all,
    my maverick daughters?..

Come Day, Go Day

Summer gave way to Autumn... slow surrender.
One leaf-falling day Ann hurried down from the hall:

- *That was Jenny on the phone... She – they've been thinking.... Mulling over things....*

Pause

- *They – they want to, to come home...*

Pause

- *Things haven't worked out and they, they're sorry about... It would be just for a little while until...*
- *No... No way.*
- *Ah! How can you sit there and say that?!*
- *No, problem –*
- *Your own flesh and blood!..*
- *I've had it – up to here!*
- *We all do mad things when we're young – or don't you remember?*
- *I don't recall ever breaking anyone's heart – least of all my parents.*
- *This – this isn't the Sean I know - married.*
- *Brat. Brats!*
- *What?!*

As the weeks passed unease set in: edginess, restlessness, impatience, the urge to move on, out, explore yet again, see "what's out there" one last time. 'Away from Dad leaning on them, Ann's quiet routine… (*'My way is best'*)

Sad. And sadder still when the move was not to New York or Berlin, Croatia or Melbourne – but to a few streets away from the family home, to house-sharing with fellow rebels they had met up with along the way - downhill.

Ash tray?.. 'Must be one somewhere - the ad said fully furnished…Use a saucer for now. Or a mug… Tissues?. There's half a toilet roll in the…

A disco on their night off… Or stay in on *'Broke Nights'* - rent a video, ring the Pizza place, chip in, scramble the price before the delivery guy pulls up at 99 No Hopeville.

End of the month, rent looming… Bum a few bob here, a fiver there...

'Get it back to you as soon as… Ah, you're a brick, Hal!'

Oh, Jenny, Jenny…
What are ye at, at all, at all,
my maverick daughters?..

Come Day, Go Day

Summer gave way to Autumn… slow surrender.
One leaf-falling day Ann hurried down from the hall:

- That was Jenny on the phone… She – they've been thinking…. Mulling over things….

Pause

- They – they want to, to come home…

Pause

- Things haven't worked out and they, they're sorry about… It would be just for a little while until…
- No… No way.
- Ah! How can you sit there and say that?!
- No, problem –
- Your own flesh and blood!..
- I've had it – up to here!
- We all do mad things when we're young – or don't you remember?
- I don't recall ever breaking anyone's heart – least of all my parents.
- This – this isn't the Sean I know - married.
- Brat. Brats!
- What?!

- 'All they are! Selfish, self centered, what's-in-it-for-them takers!
- Well, if that's all you –
- No, look, let me – People around here know me, neighbours know the score. Those two girls have shamed – embarrassed me –
- I know how you –
- You don't know the half of it!.. I drive past their college ever so often - where they were enrolled not all that long ago… I see girls, scores of them, uniformed – Inter, Leaving cert – and I think what could have, might have – I burn up inside!
- So they didn't fit in – that doesn't mean they're failures!
- Failures? They are disasters!
- You don't see it, do you? So they were outside the loop… square peg, round hole… But they have so much else going for them -
- Like what? –
- What counts! Have it in spades! If there was an honours degree in personality they'd fly it! Charm? The birds in the trees aren't safe!.. And they have what many a girl in that school hasn't got –
- Tell me.
- They speak well. Just that. Make themselves heard, understood. I'll give their mother that, she taught them how to talk – deliver… No one ever has to say - 'What?.. Sorry?.. Come again.''
- And how far will that get them in the big, bad world?
- They'll surprise you, Sean, give us all a lift! They'll do well, I just know they will!.. 'Take our breath away!

Winning ways, they have, that'll stand to them all their lives... Make their Dad so proud!..
- That'll be the day –
- And there's a thing, Sean; they love you... love their Dad... For all your faults and failings – all the mood swings – they love you...
They want to try again... us to help them... And if that means we have to try again, too... well... I'm willing...

She waited... determined as ever.

- Did... did they say when they want to, to move? -
- They'll ring...
- When... when they're ready...
- Yes?..
- I... I'll... drive down... pick them up...

And so it was – the Comeback Kids came again and Dad gets in line – at the bathroom...

Square Peg One

Easy does it. No post mortem. Accusation. Recrimination… Later… when the dust had settled… I approached -

Hi… Here's something that might be up your alley… An ad in today's paper:

"Trinity college… A two-year course in Theatre Studies… Applicants wishing to apply…"

And here's a thing, Jenny – before you start throwing the head – acceptance based on Audition, only. Get it? Have a think about it, okay? Let me know what you – what? No. No fees. Well, there's no mention of money…

Look, they just want to know if you've got what it takes… Acting. Different voices. Improvising. Y'know, making it up as you go along… Telling a story…

Well, you're forever going round the house when you think no one's listening, trying out different accents, giving your sister the giggles, asking for her assurance, reassurance… This could be the makings of you, girl…

- Dad… could I have that add?
- Sure… I cut it out soon as I… Here.

Square Peg Two

Hi... I've been thinking... Spotted this in the paper just the other day... Vacancies... A day college in town, secretarial course starting soon... Typing, filing, reception, office, 'phone, taking calls – that sort of thing...
No, it doesn't say anything about academic –
Well, you've got to do something, girl – 'just can't hang about... This, this course might just give you an opening – help you land a job.

Sure, yes, I've shared with Ann; we both think it would be a good idea and yes, we will pay the fees. Up front. So we'd need you to tell us that you're willing to try... this time really try... We'd feel right fools – throwing good money after bad...

Five day week. Nine to four… Get you out of the house. Make new friends, your own age… And some evenings you could try getting up to speed on my computer*… Okay?

* (My very first P C. Huge. Cumbersome. Clank, clunk. A monster by comparison with today's devices!..)

Square Peg One

- *Dad!.. Dad?!*
- *What?*
- *I've heard from Trinity, Dad! They've given me a time and a date!*
- *For, for interview?*
- *For audition, Dad! Audition!*
- *Great. Well done… Calm, calm down, Jenny, okay?.. There's a way to go yet…*
- *I can't believe it, Dad! Oh, Dad, I am so, so —*
- *So is that all, just show up, they'll call the shots?..*
- *'Seems so… One thing, though, I have to do a monologue from a play by a modern playwright…*
- *So… no big deal… An hour in the local library and you should come up with a goodie or two…*
- *Dad..?*
- *Yes?*

- *I was wondering...*
- *What?*
- *If – if you'd let me use your, your monologue...*
- *Huh?!*
- *The, The McMaster Piece.*
- *You're joking!*
- *No, honest! I love it, Dad – loved it the first time I read it...*
- *Well, I –*
- *Please, Dad. I would feel so comfortable doing it – it would be half the battle. And I'd be so proud...*
- *Hmmm... There's a thing.*
- *Sorry?..*
- *I was just going back over it the other day – a snip here, wee edit there. Stronger now, leaner. Tell you what: I'll print a copy when I've been over it one last time – so you can make it your own...*
- *Oh, Dad! I am so – ! I could hug you this minute!*
- *Well, what's stopping you? 'Better than sulking...*
- *Oh, Dad, Dad... And it was you that spotted that ad – only for you I wouldn't have known!*
- *Well, I -*
- *Dear, darling Dad... My Dad, aren't you?*

(A lad growing up in a small town in Ireland after WW 2... two or three cinemas ('picture houses')... no TV, video... no mobiles... grim. Rationing still in place... "So when the fit-ups came to town some of us were fit to be tied!..")

The McMaster Piece

I was into plays and all like that at school.
And the Brothers knew it.
One day Brother O'Toole walked in -
I was in Fifth Year, taking it easy -
and called me out.

I was sure I was in for it but it wasn't that at all.
There was this company of players
coming to the Town to do Shakespeare
and all like that
and they wanted a lad that'd be interested
for crowd scenes and walk-ons.
I only leapt at it!

That evening I was round to the hall
and shown into the presence:
God he was tall!
Loch of blonde hair, blue eyes
and a boom of a voice:

Anew McMaster.

Not that I ever got talking to him.
He was way above me.
Just stood there, 'me mouth open...

They were opening with Romeo and Juliet.
When the time came I was led round
and up onto the stage,
a sword put in me hand.
'Crowded. This fella facing me.

"What do I do?" says I. *"
When the curtain goes up,"*
says he, *"start fighting..."*

A kick-start to a wondrous season!
I was a soldier in MacBeth,
a mariner in Othello,
another citizen in the Merchant of Venice,
one of the chorus in Oedipus Rex
when he came on again at the end,
the eyes out of his head!..
Oh, I didn't half get a fright!

Towards the end of the run
Mac said they were going on a tour
to Australia and would I like to come?
Ah, like that. Australia!

But the father and the mother said no,
get your Leaving first,
you won't get anywhere
without your Leaving.

So off they went and I bent
over the handle bars
into another winter of
east winds and short days
and everything through Irish…

All my life I followed the safe way.
Sure, you have to be more than a bit mad
to take a chance,
go out on a limb,
step off the end of the pier…
Still, I… I sometimes wonder…
how it would have… how I might have…
if I had… if only…

It's something I've been meaning to tell
the young ones:
Not to be afraid to, to go for it,
give it your best shot
while the years are still on your side…

'Few years ago - ah, it's a good few now -
I read in the paper where he died. Mac.
End of Act One, huh?
They're very lucky to have him:
He'll do Shakespeare for God Almighty
and all his angels and saints for saecula…

The day after they were gone
I went round to the Library above
and took out The Merchant of Venice.
"Many a time and oft on the Rialto…"

I kept at it until I had it be heart.
Though I didn't know it at the time
it was a way of trying to reach
to the far ends of the earth,
keep him in mind…

I could do a fair take on him

as Shylock. I could.

'Said it to some of the local group once

but they said

I wouldn't have been right for it.

(pause)

I would have been.

(pause)

I know I would have been...

Hmmm…

A male monologue as part of her presentation?! And what will the panel make of that?

  - The McMaster Piece, eh?
  - Dick's lines at the end of a black comedy -
  - By?
  - Sean Walsh… He's my Dad.
  - Hmmm… (The plot thickens.)

- So... How long have you got, Jenny?
- A week from today... 'Nerves, Dad. Bag o' nerves!
- If you weren't nervous you wouldn't be worth a damn!..
- I'll have that hug now…

The Keyboard Kid

Wonders will never cease! Jenny! Stay in? Evenings? Nights? You're joking!.. A grenade in the hall? She'd jump over it and away out with her… And had an excuse for every night of the week - and a few extra for the weekends!

Greta's birthday party… I promised Carmel that I'd help her with… Dermot is leaving to go to… Missus Rafferty's in a bad way – the nerves are at her - I told Angela I'd…

And quite the expert at juggling - endless variations concocted on the spot, effortlessly… 'Going out' the bottom line - impulsive, compelling, addictive…

But then, as she leaned into the secretarial course, I began to notice a change: lo and behold, she actually stayed in some weekday evenings… lingering a while at the table in the dining room – where I had anchored the Monster… Showing an interest… toying with keys… buttons... experimenting… trying one thing, then another…

But still prone to answer when the phone rang in the hall: chatting with one girl friend or another, endlessly… To me, small talk; to her, of serious importance…

Look, Jenny… I have to say, I'm up there in my space, trying to write. 'Like, I hear the sound of it – bugs after a while… So will you please ease up a bit, get your friends to phone earlier? Eh-hh?
Or I'll never get to finish the script I'm working on…

That last sentence did it. My daughters were avidly interested in what I was trying to create on blank paper. Almost overnight, the phone calls ceased…

And I have to say she kept her work station neat, tidy – whatever about her bedroom! Yet another indicator the course was beginning to show results. And careful to switch off the machina when she had done for the night.

I was just turning away when I noticed a single sheet of paper protruding from the back of her A4 pad. I eased it out – noting Jenny's careful hand - began to read… froze… stood riveted as the penny dropped… then slumped into a chair, gobsmacked…
And that's how Ann found me:

- Sean? Sean, time to pack it in for the…What? What is it?
I handed her the page… waited as she read it.

- Yours?
- It's a lift from the script I'm working on! 'Get it? It means she opened a file that was none of her business!

- Well, I –
- How dare she! How bloody dare she!.. The little so-n-so!.. And she gave me her word, I trusted her! Keyboard only. As often as you want, much as you – but don't meddle with my stuff! And she did, bloody did!
- Well, you must have known her curiosity would get the better of her? The two of them always mad to know what you're at!
- Tomorrow. Soon as I get the chance, I'll have it out with her –
- Tell her how you came across that page, poking around her –
- What?
- The very thing you'll be accusing her of, her Dad has it in spades -
- Oh, I –
- I'm away to bed. Let you do the same – after you've read that page again – without anger…
- What?
- God only knows how much she read but this caught her eye, she wrote it down – to keep it, maybe show her sister…
- I, I wasn't thinking that –
- Leave her be, Sean… Let it go… Sleep on it. You'll see in the morning I'm right… She loves you… that page proves it. 'Very much…

As she closed the door behind her
I began to read anew:

*"Ah, the best I can... 'Not easy, to be honest with you.
I'm not much of a parent, even at the best of times.
And at the worst I, I can be a holy terror.*

*Well, like, coming the heavy... Or letting her down...
Raising my voice - maybe even giving the odd roar...
I mean, if there's a sin at all on my soul I'd like lifted,
it's the way I go on at times with my young one...*

I will, Father. I'll try again..."

Lines from the confessional sequence… part of the work that was then still in its infancy… growing, changing, morphing, maturing… trying one way, then another… experimenting… searching, betimes, for a light at the end of a very dark tunnel…

'Little knowing that it would one day see the light of day as an Amazon paperback... with a title that only came to me after some scratching and scraping on blank paper… leaving me, for one, quite stunned...

Amazon.com ebook, paperback. Smashwords.com

Night Prayer

Dear Ann,
I found this healing prayer in my bag this morning; it was given to me in hospital by one of the old ladies and because it is so powerful I thought you would benefit from it at this time.

More than that though, I think it would help Dad to sleep better at night, it could help him to release all the painful memories that have him so tormented.

Jesus, through the power of the Holy Spirit,
go back into my memory as I sleep.
Every hurt that has ever been done to me…
heal that hurt.

Every hurt that I have ever caused
to another person…heal that hurt.

All the relationships that have been damaged
in my whole life that I am not aware of…
heal those relationships.

But Lord, if there is anything that I need to do…
if I need to go to a person because he is still
suffering from my hand…
bring to my awareness that person.

I choose to forgive, and I ask to be forgiven.
Remove whatever bitterness
may be in my heart, Lord,
and fill the empty spaces with your Love.

Thank you, Jesus… Amen.

Isn't it beautiful?..

God bless...

Love.

Jenny.

**As you are... beautiful!
Jenny Big Heart...**

Jesus, through the power of the Holy Spirit,
go back into my memory as I sleep.
Every hurt that has ever been done to me…
heal that hurt.

Every hurt that I have ever caused
to another person…heal that hurt.

All the relationships that have been damaged
in my whole life that I am not aware of…
heal those relationships.

But Lord, if there is anything that I need to do…
if I need to go to a person because he is still
suffering from my hand…
bring to my awareness that person.

I choose to forgive, and I ask to be forgiven.
Remove whatever bitterness
may be in my heart, Lord,
and fill the empty spaces with your Love.

Thank you, Jesus… Amen.

Isn't it beautiful?..

God bless...

Love.

Jenny.

**As you are... beautiful!
Jenny Big Heart...**

Dad! Dad, I got it!
I'm on the Course, Dad!

As I reckoned… Not that I had money on it – I was never a betting man – but I had this hunch, almost from the word Go, that she would fly it… If ever a candidate showed potential! 'The promise of a rich Spring-tide.

'Much hugging and hand clapping, hurrahs a plenty… Champagne? Well, no, not yet, not quite yet… But at the end of the two years ahead, all going to plan, I might just invest in a case or two!..

'Bring her back down to earth? What! 'Day One of Dream Come Through?.. Not a hope!.. But as the start of the course drew near I made a quiet approach:

***Anyone ever tell you, girl**, you're a rough diamond? Well, that's about what you are this minute! When a diamond comes out of the earth it's not up to much but clean it, polish it again and again, and just watch it glow!..*

And look, let me just say - It doesn't just happen, you have to make it happen… You'll get as much out of this course as you put – Jenny? Jenny, are you listening to a word I'm saying?!

'Faraway eyes. Ah, that's enough… But maybe – just maybe – when she comes back to earth on the morrow she will remember that her Dad is backing her… all the way.

Success!

So Jenny Younger has a cert, diploma, parchment… 'To whom it may concern… in case she's ever asked… Well good for her! 'Made it, got there! And her final report: *ability to adopt, take the initiative…* Oh, well done, Jenny!

- Now hang on, man! We're not talking University degree!..

- I know, I know. But don't you see? For that wee girl it was climbing Everest; me watching her ascent!

Of course I had to make a meal of it! Sure I had! If only to make some sort of amends for the times in the past I had put her down, knocked her first efforts, fumbling attempts, at creativity…

Me that should have known better! 'Dismissed when I was her age – first attempts at a poem, short story, scene from a play in the making – a whole scene! – ridiculed by the elders in my own family. Leaving me scarred, embarrassed, wishing the ground would… So:

Buoyant Jenny! Jubilant! Her Dad and Ann so proud of her! Hugs and kisses as she sallied forth in search of a job – any job! And yes, she scored – almost from day one!

Not much of an assignment but still… A beginning, a foot on the first rung, an opportunity to prove herself… And that she did! So much so she was able to secure a better posting within a year.

And a year after that, a further move… ever upwards, her confidence growing apace… And I couldn't help noticing it was the oral that seemed to clinch it for her every time.

But then! When I heard she had answered an ad for a post in a semi-State body I choked, coughed, flustered!

Is she mad or what?! 'Academic qualifications? Irish – oral, written? 'Not a hope! She's heading for a fall – her first rejection...

Jenny Younger

"To the most wonderful mother
a girl could ask for.

Thank you so much for your love, your loyalty,
support and friendship.

I would be lost without you
and am so grateful
for the beautiful relationship we have.

Love you, Ann.
All my love.

Jenny. XXXX"

Ann came down from the hall,

triumphant bearer of good news:

"That was Jenny on the phone – she got it!.."

I'll Go On…

Jenny, now in her second year at Trinity, came home one evening and presented me with a framed photo/card:

in the far distance, an old man, stooped and wearing a bowler hat on bowed head, struggles with baggage; while near at hand a man with protruding ears sits with his back to us, darkly, framing the inscription:

NO MATTER - TRY AGAIN - FAIL AGAIN - FAIL BETTER…

Beckett. Ah, yes. The Master. Words of wisdom, encouragement, inspiration…

My daughter knew I was creatively under the weather - fumbling, stumbling, not knowing where I was going, how the story-line would work out…

As has happened to me on several occasions in the past, I did find my way, finally – and took it… The script went on to cause considerable ripples when produced, broadcast.

And Beckett's framed dictat? To this day it stands on my desk, to the left of my desktop P C, at the edge of the arc of light from my reading lamp.

I look at it now and again… whenever I get bogged down, dispirited – and keep going.

The Graduate

Taken by a professional photographer. A pose? But of course! Not a bit like the girl who romps around in jeans and jumper. But still...

It was her big day, her hour of triumph. We were justly proud of her, as were some friends, country cousins... A hush when she came on stage in costume - a demo piece of melodrama... Applause! Applause!

Then *the few words* from a man in a gown before we adjourned to a pub across from Trinity and a final toast: *Here's Looking at You, Kid!..*

Not so much **Up, Up and Away** as Pack Up, Set Up, Fit Up, Fed Up, End Up in the cold light of dawn at the end of a country-wide tour – playing to mostly empty houses an undemanding part in a play well removed from the few who put in an appearance.

And then there was that TV commercial! 'Turned out to be a long way from Glamourville. Setting up... take after take... hanging about... trying one thing, then another... unto wrap-up.

And – more than likely – clean out of cigarettes! Her peer group dissolved... companions of Yesteryear gone their different ways... No more pubbing at weekends, chipping in, fingers crossed the kitty would last... Endless, gushing conversations, great good humour, a stout camaraderie that drew to a final curtain all too soon...

It was about this time (!) Jenny decided it was not the life for her; 'opted instead for a husband, the assurance of a home, the prospect of family…

And though I wasn't consulted at all – 'bugged me at the time – her decision gave me much relief.

Flashback – in Wonder…

When she took off I gave her a month. She'll be back, 'bet any money! London'll cure her cough!..

But the weeks passed. And the seasons. She hung in there, held out, roughing it. But kept in touch - the occasional letter, the so seldom phone call...

And then… then there was this: I keep it here in the middle drawer. Her writ – not mine…

Dad, I can't start listing off all the things I did wrong before I left home. We both know how wrong I was and now I am sorry.

More than anything I would like to talk to you, to sort this mess out, to tell you from my heart how sorry I am, how much I really love you and miss you, as my Dad.

Please take this letter as being sincere. I need you, Dad, in my life. Please don't block me out.
I know I pushed you away, or rather I ran away from you.

One thing I will always regret is that I never put my pride aside and asked for your advice on my plans, or indeed advice on anything... I love you, Dad... I'm so sorry...

I want you to know that I still say my prayers and go to Mass on Sunday. Well, not every Sunday, to be honest. But nearly every... See, I won't tell you a lie. That day's over.

And if I do miss Mass I say a few extra prayers during the week. Especially the one you taught me - the Serenity Prayer... And I still have that card you gave me when I was leaving: It's up on the wall over my bed, place of honour...

Footprints

And sometimes I think that's me walking along the sea shore, side by side with Jesus. Two sets of foot prints... And after a while I look back and see only one set... And I turn to Jesus and say - "Why did you leave me, Lord, when I most needed you?"
And Jesus answers – "I didn't leave you, Jenny. When the going got really rough I carried you..."

But Dad, what makes me swallow my fears and keep going is knowing that at long last you are proud of me and at the end of the day that's worth more than gold dust.

Now you and I are friends, Dad, great friends. We can just talk normally to one another and I adore it. I love you completely, Dad. Sometimes when we have been speaking on the phone or I get a letter from you, I could just burst with the love I have for you... I love you, Dad. Love you to bits. And always will. No matter what...   - Jenny.

Hmmm... Follow that, huh?.. And she does, I do believe she does. Deep down... Even loves, betimes, my very inadequacy, hopelessness. 'Like the day she glanced up at me, frowning, from the Pets' Column in the evening paper to ask –

Dad, what's a rough collie? Like, why is it called rough?

I hadn't a clue... Stammered... blurted... *Eh-hhh... Well, like... y'know... the way they go –* 'Ruff! Ruff!'

The look on her face! Incredulity giving way to irrepressible mirth!..

I'll be home for Christmas, *Dad, for sure...*
Wild horses wouldn't stop me!..
But this time I'll be home to be home!
"Sleep all day, stay out half the night?"
Not any more!

Oh, look up a few old friends, sure,
but I'll be around that much
you'll think you're being haunted!..

And I'll make the stuffing and cook the dinner…
And I'll decide what programs we watch, okay?..
Okay. that's cool…

Home

'Few days at Christmas… A week in summer –
if she can manage the fare… But never again
to call home our home,
no matter how warm the hearth,
how welcoming the arms…

London, eh... The Enveloper...

*'Only Adoption Society known to
many's an Irish lad and lassie.*

*Will she put down roots then?
'Family in suburbia - or wherever...
Weens spouting the Queen's English –
clipping vowels, mincing consonants –
in pace with the tempo of the great
Get-Up-and-Go...*

*'Knowing little - caring even less –
about a rich heritage this side of the sea.*

(No! Please God, no...)

From London... with Love

Dear Dad,
I want very much to tell you how I feel about US, to ask you to try to see things from my point of view. I loved my room at the top of the house, Dad. You gave it to me when we first moved in and I loved it. It really was mine. My room...

I used to look out the attic window a lot, not just to have a smoke - but to look around me. 'At the mountains on a clear day, at the sky...

Dad, you never encouraged me to watch TV and I never really felt comfortable being downstairs. So I would bring my coffee and biscuits back up to my room and shut the door and get on with it.

I'd turn on a tape and sing, or I would take out some paper and paint or I would read or write letters, and occasionally I did some study...

And downstairs didn't belong in my room.

So you could be in the foulest of moods and it ceased to matter, anymore, when I was up there.

You had your golf and your pub pals and your newspapers and the television programs you wanted to watch - mostly the news and the weather forecast...

I had my room and it was up there I made up my mind to leave. So that I could just do what I wanted, when and how I wanted, and the only person I had to justify it to was myself and God.

Dad, I used to wish sometimes that you would leave me be. I wish that you could have said to me -"Have a good time" when I was skulking out. Or asked me if I had written any good poems lately or whatever...

I just wished that when we sat down and talked it wasn't only for you to tell me to study, to stay in, to take down my posters... You didn't want to know about aspects of my life that to you seemed trivial but were to me very important.

And, like you are, Dad, it wasn't easy to sit back and let go a little, give me a bit of slack. And although when I left home you wouldn't speak to me for ages and that hurt - hurt, hurt! - I wouldn't let on for a minute that it did. But I wouldn't wish it on anybody. The fears, the uncertainties...

And even now, after all this time, when things are going badly and I'm feeling down, the only place on this earth I want to be is at home, in my room, and you there to say to me that everything will be all right.

Dad, you are a great father, you really are. And I know you were hurt, hurt terribly, when Mum took off - though you tried the best you could not to show it, to me, anyhow, maybe me above all.

And for all our rows and falling-outs, I loved you, Dad, loved you the sun, moon and stars.

Don't ask me to explain, I couldn't. It's what I feel, not what I know...

I'll post this now, spelling mistakes and all! If it helps clear the air, fair enough. If not, at least I can say - I gave it my best shot! And that's something else you taught me...

- Jenny.

Dad, hold me! Don't let me –
Oh, Jenny, Jenny Alana...
I held on to you as long as I...
And when the time came
it was you that let go of me.
But sure, that's how it is...
that's the way of it...

Dad, I have to tell you, when Mum took off it ripped the heart out of me, it really did...

Hmmm... 'Think you were the only one? 'Lots of kids, lots of broken homes, this day and age... 'Learnt to live with it, take it on the chin...

Your friend, Brenda, did all right for herself, right? 'Father died when she was a ween, her mother an alco, off the wall...

Shane in the next row survived - and he had to contend with breakdown, split... a rented house in town... a new and officious mother... All right?..

No, it wasn't all right, Dad!..

It wasn't Brenda or Shane or whoever - it was me. Me!

And if they coped, fine, great. But I didn't - couldn't...

One of my teachers said my face was a mask – how right she was!..

Oh, I did try, at least at first - to pay attention, listen, take it in – but sure, half the time I wasn't there: inside was churning...

Dad... Dad, you never encouraged *me to watch TV -*

That's right, I didn't. Didn't! 'Switched it off, more often than not - to facilitate you, inconvenience me!.. I did it for you, can't you see that? The box was the enemy, destroyer of concentration, application!

So I would bring my coffee and biscuits back up to my room and shut the door and downstairs didn't belong in my room. I'd turn on a tape and sing, or I would take out some paper and paint or I would read or write letters, and sometimes I did some study...

Sometimes?.. Sometimes!..

Well, as long as you didn't overdo it!..

That wasn't the deal, kiddo... You were up there to keep the head down - for the most part. 'Not moon in a mirror, gawk out the window, arse around...

One thing I will always regret is that I never put my pride aside and asked for your advice on my plans, or indeed advice on anything... I'm so sorry...

Now you and I are friends, Dad, great friends. We can just talk normally to one another and I adore it. I love you completely, Dad.

Sometimes when we have been speaking on the phone or I get a letter from you, I could just burst with the love I have for you...

I love you, Dad. Love you to bits. And always will. 'No matter what...

Jenny.

As You Grow Older...

You learn the subtle difference
between holding a hand and chaining a soul

And you learn that love doesn't mean leaning
and company doesn't mean security

And you begin to learn that kisses aren't contracts
and presents aren't promises

And you begin to accept your defeats with
your head up and your eyes open -

with the grace of a woman,
not the grief of a child

And you learn to build all your roads
on Today
because Tomorrow's ground is too
uncertain for plans
and futures have
a way of falling down in mid-flight

After a while you learn that even sunshine
burns if you get too much

So plant your own garden and decorate
your own soul
instead of waiting
for someone to bring you flowers

And you learn that you really can endure
that you really are strong.

And that you really do have worth,
and you learn and you learn...

With every goodbye you learn.

(Author? Wish I knew...)

Come in, Jenny Three!

Welcome! Welcome!.. They broke my heart, then put the pieces together again - better than ever!

Sunday lunch… brunch.
The fare? Yummy. The craic? 'Ninty!
And the jug of water?.. To die for!

To the very special lady in my life:

I want to wish you the happiest of birthdays

but I also want to thank you today

for your love, friendship and loyalty –

for always, always, having faith in me.

We are blessed to have you

and to be loved by you.

'Happy birthday, dearest Ann.

*"I hope that you put on paper
all that has happened in your life,
even though it would probably hurt you,
and then probably your soul
would begin to heal,
and the rest of the world
would have a great play to see!!"*

January 1991.
Siobhan's birthday card to her Dad, last par.

'Not just the ice cream that's melting...

Older than Joanna, she maybe found it that bit harder to accept the new status quo.

'Let go of Yesterday, welcome Today - and the promise of a better Tomorrow...

And no one realised it more than Ann. 'Took a while... 'Not easy. Apart, at first, they grew gradually closer. And Siobhan came to accept, love Ann: Godsend.

'**At me to** drop in some day – whenever. So…

At Reception, smiles as soon as I mentioned her name:
the vibe was good, Joanna was well got.
A quick call and she was down in a heart beat –
to whisk me up a flight of stairs, then around to her office.

Well, hi! What? Oh, wow?! I don't believe - !?

Organised Jo! Files to hand. Desk in order, neat.
She smiled, sensing my wonderment, pride…
Then the phone rang:
"Hello… Joanna here… How can I help you?.."

Warm. Clear. Receptive. Interested. Concerned…
Will she be kept? They'd be mad not to!

Oh, sure, lovely. A heart warmer…

But tread carefully, Sean!
Remember that day Way Back When –
when you frowned at Joanna,
passed a remark that displeased her?..

She pulled a face, left the table,
went in search of Big Sister…
tears, whispers. Then both to Ann, urgently.

"WHAT?!!"

Me, quite unaware…
Suddenly all three were in the door
and at me, shrilling.

*All right! Sorry. Sorry, Joanna…
Didn't mean to…!*

'Hands up… Remember? I'll never forget!

**Under scrutiny…
Approach with caution!**

'Like to get between them?

Be my guest!

Not Hi Steria all the time – not at all…

When they fight it's bullets for breakfast.

But if a third party enters the arena?

To intrude, intervene –

no matter how well intentioned:

Take no prisoners!..

Catch Up, one of several, over the years. A fun thing. Jokes, quips, laughter, light hearted banter… But surface stuff. 'Nothing serious. No real depth. I allowed myself to be steered – instead of steering.

So… deep breath… and:

'You think I was never like you, never your age? 'God's sake! I went with the flow, no bother! Smoker… drinker… pubs and parties… Sure, you weren't a man at all if you hadn't a fag in one hand, a glass in the other! Aye, and ready to bawl with the rest of them – Ireland, boys, hurray!' - or brawl at the drop of a hat?..

'Took me years of half-living before it even began to dawn on me: is this it?.. 'this all there is?.. Why am I saying this? Now! Putting a damper on the evening? Could it not have waited, I hear you say?
Let me answer: Love...

I don't want you to go the Way of the Many... fall into the same trap as those ahead in the queue. I wish you Life, not Death. Seriously...

You're waving me away, putting me down? It could never happen to you! No way are you in the least bit alcoholic...
No? Wanna bet?
The man takes the bottle, the bottle takes the man –
or woman...

Habit... habit forming... unto addiction. 'Can jump up and bite you in the neck when you're least expecting...

A wino lying in the gutter nursing a bottle of plonk, that your idea/image of an alcoholic? Ha!.. Maybe yes, maybe no – 'hurdly adequate...

Bear with me – here's the best – the very best definition of alcoholism I have ever come across.

**If your drinking over a period of time –
say, several months –
has had a detrimental effect on your life:
work… social… family… health… love life,
then you, darling, you are an alcoholic.**

No shame, please, no cause for blushing! The shame is in denial, bluffing, blustering… in deflection… transfer of guilt… lying, manipulation… protesting innocence while riddled with guilt…

Claiming responsibility, maturity while knowing damn-well you have been quite, quite irresponsible, immature, in the not-so-distant past!

*No shame in crying out for help when feeling hopeless, helpless, in thrall to an unyielding addiction…
No shame in grabbing, holding on for dear life, to a life-line thrown from a safe embankment by a sympathetic Samaritan…*

Takes courage, the determination of the Desperate,
to go, get there, take a seat among the Recovering –
but never destined to be fully recovered...

Listen while one, then another - the old and
the old-before-their-time - tell how
they hit Skid Row, struggled to their feet,
began to claw their way back up the sheer face
of a merciless cliff...

No shame in standing, praying together,
united in mortal combat:
"God... grant me Serenity..."

But I didn't, did I?.. No, not a word... Better not, eh?..
'Might well do more harm than good.

Genes, do y'see... all down to the genes.
No way of telling what way a young one will turn out,
what legacy is there beneath the surface?..

A medic once assured me:
"Anything – anything – can happen in alcohol..."

And a wise man counseled me – too late, alas –
"Never make a decision when you're drinking…"

But at least I can share - try to share -
a favourite prayer with my daughters,
hoping that they will copy, file…
one day take to heart,
share with their own offspring,
whenever…

Dear God.

Enlighten what is dark in me
Strengthen what is weak in me
Mend what is broken in me
Bind what is bruised in me
Heal what is sick in me
and lastly,
Revive whatever peace and love
has died in me…

Centre Circle

*"A long walk down a short corridor
into a circle of strangers –
Emma across from me, strangest of them all."*

My ebook. When I published on **Amazon Kindle** and **Smashwords.com** I received the following lines, penned by *Kieran*... 'A pen name or the first name of a real correspondent? I cannot say – but I have no reason to doubt the veracity of the writer. (As written, no edits…)

*"That's an accurate account of the life of an Alcoholic. I know well the madness of the Walking Wounded - ducking in and out of sobriety, detoxing for a fortnight, then bingeing for another eternity, until by circumstance forced - and physically crippled - to quit again!
It's a hellish 'disease.'
I immediately checked out your other writings and liked the open, honest and uncomplicated nature of your style. I will be keeping a keen eye out for future postings. Your imagery is clear and inspiring. Good luck."*

She breezed in the front door: *"Now Ann and Dad, I'm off work all next week, staying at home, so if there's anything – anything at all – I can do for you, you only have to…"*

She waited, treading water. Straight faced, I volleyed back at her: *"Well if you'd sort out my filing, I'd be ever so…"*

Brake! Change gear! Smile running down chin… She had often been in my space off the first landing: folders on the floor, scripts piled high, files stuffed with MSS, books stacked every which way, memos, receipts, discs - all encased in an ancient layer of fine dust…

"No… No, Dad… I won't do your filing…"
She looked at me, taken aback, as I laughed outright.
"Don't mind him, Joanna. He's only winding you up."

'Ann at her side… ever on her side …

*Yes, you can! Yes you can, too! My darling daughter…
Those poems you showed me – I saw at once the promise!
And as I lauded them I swear you lifted from the ground!
At table, when you asked me to read one or two aloud,
the response from Jo and Ann was warmly spontaneous!*

*Yes, you can – write! Look, your letters from London, back a
bit: do you think for one moment I would have included them
in my book if they were not up to par? Not at all, no way!
They are there because they read so very well, from the
heart, love letters out of the ordinary…*
*Written by a girl in exile, pining for home, who had no
notion that they would ever see the light of day in one of her
Dad's published writs!*

Forgive me if I have caused offence – I mean well.
Intended to give my daughter encouragement,
heaps of much needed self confidence,
the will and determination to try and keep trying.

To banish – and forever – fear of failure…
of rejection… of sneering, jeering, put-downs.

And oh, how I'd love you to record your words,
spoken to camera – your voice, your poetry…

Ritual

My father standing in the kitchen,
peeling an orange.
'So engrossed, I can watch unobserved.

He is careful, methodical. There is no rush.
He holds the orange in both hands.
A gentle massage - or a prayer in thanks, maybe? –
before he opens the skin with his thumb.

Then the removal of the pith.
Piece by piece he carefully pulls it away,
placing it, gently, atop the peelings
on the kitchen counter.
'Every bit of it discarded
before the consuming can begin.

And now, the dividing:
a segment here, two segments there -
and always he will come to where I am sitting
and place some pieces before me.

> An offering of sorts. I am honoured.
> The peeling of an orange:
> a holy ritual in my father's hands.
>
> *- Siobhan Walsh Flanagan.*

Yes, Siobhan! Indeed, yes! You can…
Then do. Write. Every day without fail.
For a start *have a go at your old man, lacerate him*
for daring to publish pages of yours without
as much as by your leave or would it be all right if?..
'Should read quite well, that – I reckon!

Write rubbish. Write better rubbish… You cannot edit
an empty page – or a blank screen… Sometimes
in the debris you'll unearth a rough stone in need of
cleansing, polishing, shining… unto ruby glow.
Then to it! But not at once… 'Only when you've
quite forgotten, can look at it anew, as might a stranger…

What to write?! Come on! You've lived half a life span,
your mind a reservoir of memories that only you
can recall, record, write out, distil…

Joanna! Again and again to the rescue when Ann or I
came unstuck, trying to deal with one eventuality or another.
Like when I came up against a stone wall, on-line, bogged
down on one site or another –
she called after work, sat down at my desktop
and had me sorted in jig time.

My very own P R O
And when it came to organising the Launch
of my very first Paperback – *Notes on the Past Imperfect* –
at the Writers Centre, she was a super support…
Invitations, the guest list, handouts, phone calls,
posters, photos, display board, sales…
wines, soft drinks, finger food - why she even had
our G P on hand with his upmarket camera!

And how proud she was of her Dad when he ended
"the few words" and bowed out to applause…

Siobhan: Tough Love, Smoker!

Surrey, England. The start of the 70's. Night.
Suddenly awake, jerked back to the surface by a lightening bolt – *You're out of fags, Sean!*
What? Oh, no?..
Oh, yes!..
'Must be some mistake, I always keep two or three for morning, no matter what…
Well, this time, no, lad – you don't have a cigarette to your name. So just turn over, get back to sleep and –

No!..

What! What are you doing?
What does it look like? I'm up, trying to get into a pair of trousers, fumbling in the dark, no lights, not wanting to wake the house…

'Downstairs. Kitchen light. Counting loose change. Making sure I had enough coins for a dispensing machine – if I can find one…
You're not going out at this – ?!
Shut up! Just shut the Hell up!..

Overcoat. Keys. Ease open the front door, pull it quietly closed… Off at a lively pace, downhill: *a mind-locked addict, desperate for a fix…*

After a long, long walk came upon a dispensing machine at a shop entrance – closed. On then, further… another tiring walk, another dispenser – again closed… Forcing myself forward, another punishing mile… almost crying, despairing… giving in, up…

Oh, there! Look! And this time, this time!..
I fumbled with coins, dropping one, not bothering to look for it in the dark, dropping the exact amount – ever so carefully - into the slot… And hey! Gotcha! Oh, the relief as a packet of twenty dropped into the tray…
Opening, urgently… cigarette to mouth… match, striking… Inhale.
Tension ebbing even as I sucked smoke deep down… exhaling, reluctantly.

Long trudge back through the town and home, uphill… Kettle… cuppa… light another… last drag… Back to bed, some sleep before facing into another day.

No exaggeration. Not the shadow of a lie… That really did happen.

Worse to come! Years – oh, decades – later (back in Ireland long since) Ann and I drove to Limerick for the funeral of a relative. A friend of the bereaved family had offered to put us up, overnight. We duly arrived, greeting and being greeted, and were soon upstairs, unpacking, when I reached for cigarettes and lighter. Ann –

You're not going to smoke in the - !?

I rounded on her, seething. *Would you ever f--k off!*
Shock... face draining...

First time I had ever spoken to her like that – and the last.
'Sorry as soon as the words had ripped from my lips. But still went ahead with the ritual – conceding only to do so in the adjoining bathroom, at open window...

Years later still - after recurring bouts of bronchitis, antibiotics, medics warning me of worse to come if I did not stop, word reached me that my eldest had quit. What?! I could hardly believe it!

Eldest daughter in her Dad's footsteps – addictive, compulsive, neurotic? And I knew she had tried one thing, then another, anxious – indeed, desperate – to kick it...
'Prior to anticipated pregnancy.

Came the day she rang home. I lifted the receiver, croaking, wheezing...
Sorry, love. Do - dose of laryngitis. No voice...
I waited. Then she spoke.
Forty cigarettes a day and you wonder why you have no voice?
And put down the phone.
'Stung, hurting... my pride punctured... Still, no denying the truth of her salvo...

I was out of sorts, out of pocket… miserable, depressed…In thrall to the drug, Nicotine… Next day I rang back:
Hi, Siobhan…
Hello, Dad.
Off the cigs, eh? Well done. Good for you, our lassie –

And no patch, pills, nicorette – no nothing!

So how did you – I mean, what's your secret?
Easy –
Easy?! There's nothing easy about it!
The Easy Way to Stop Smoking.
Oh…. Ann bought me a copy, 'didn't put much pass on it…
Pick it up, Dad. Read through, quickly. From cover to cover –
Well, I –
Then start again, reading slowly this time, letting wise words sink in…
Eh-hh… what have I got to lose?..
Let me know how you get on, okay?..
Okay -
And Dad?
Ah ha?..
We don't want to lose you, Dad… Your turn to give it your best shot!

So I did… But it was only when I began to read Carr's words anew, slowly, starting at page one that the penny began to drop…

We have been conditioned *to regard cigarettes as a friendly ally, crutch, support, relaxant, soother, anti-depressant –* whatever…

In actual fact, nothing could be further from the truth…
And he goes on to give the lie to each of those tags, labels…

That did it. For me. I don't like being taken for a ride at the best of times but when the scam involves ill health, discomfort, being relieved of lots of lolly… I tend to get mad!

I had been conned and I didn't like it. Not one wee bit.
It did not happen overnight, my decision to stop. But it did happen… For the first time ever I really did want to quit. 'Nothing to do with will power. Much to do with reason, seeing the sheer folly of my destructive habit…

My last night, enslaved. I took the six cigarettes that were left in the packet and broke them up, one by one, binned them… Ann watching – at my invitation – hardly believing her eyes…

Then panic! *I can't do without my crutch! I won't be able to sleep! What if I wake during the - ?*

In actual fact, I slept like a baby… Panic on awakening. A few deep breaths and hey, I feel good!.. I was on my way to freedom…

A plethora of *cures* available in shops, online. Substitute one crutch for another?! Nonsense! No pills, paste, potions, gum will kill the craving…

Use you head, keep your money!

    Do I miss them? I hate the bloody things!
     'Sicken at the smell…

**Much credit to my daughter, Siobhan!
Summer, 2001. Now into my 80's.**
Would I have made it had I kept on smoking?
(And drinking, for that matter…)
Not a hope! Not the glimmer of a vain wish!
'Dead and buried… cremated… long since.
Know what? I've never been so creative!

My thanks to Allen Carr,
may he rest in peace.

And to my daughter, Siobhan,
for her tough love…

VOCATION

"There are few callings higher than that of a writer -

so high it is fraught with peril.

Writing is not for the weak or timid.

It requires courage to face the page every day.

To send out queries that may not even be answered,

to pour yourself into a story that may or may not be read,

to lay yourself bare to a world that may only reject you."

(author unknown... to me...)

Not just sisters – friends!
Y-e-a-h!!! And for life!

Breath of Friendship

"But Oh! The blessing it is to have a friend
to whom one can speak fearlessly on any subject;
with whom one's deepest -
as well as one's most foolish thoughts -
come out simply and safely.

Oh, the comfort - the inexpressible comfort
of feeling safe with a person –
having neither to weigh thoughts
nor measure words,

but pouring them all right out,
just as they are,
chaff and grain together;
certain that a faithful hand
will take and sift them,
keep what is worth keeping,
and then
with the breath of kindness
blow the rest away."

(Dinah Maria Mulock Craik, A Life for a Life.)

I seldom quote another writer –

unless it is on target

and really hits the mark, spot on!

***Dear Ann**, I am sending you so much love today!
I think of you often. Last night, for example,
the fire was stoked and I was going to bed.
Just as I put the guard around it I thought,
Ann wouldn't waste that heat and I went and got
my clothes-horse, full of laundry, still not dry,
and wrapped it around the fire just as you always did.*

*It may seem like a small thing but it's something
you passed on to me. 'A gesture full of love and caring.
Thank you for all the small and big things
you have done for me over the years.
I love you for all of them. Thank you for making me
feel loved and minded always.*
- Siobhan.

A safe pair of hands... Molly May Flanagan, second daughter and third child of Siobhan and Benny Flanagan... with her Nana.

Dear, dearest Ann... McGarry Walsh.

Thank you for coming into our lives.
For welcoming us into your life.
For making your space our space.
Thank you for changing our way
into your... better... way.

For always being there for us –
sharing our tears and laughter,
our good days and bad...

Thank you for the buns, the scones,
the apple and rhubarb tarts...
not to mention the carrots and broccoli!

Thank you for your prayers, Scripture readings.

Thank you for being a gorgeous Granny.

Thank you for being YOU...

Siobhan, Joanna, Zoe, Charlie, Ruby, Molly.

'Finale. 'Time to start edging towards the Departure Lounge. But not before leaving a special something to my daughters by way of legacy – hoping that they will read, absorb and pass on to their children in due course... To keep and share... keep and share.

Ode to the Church

Carlo Carretto.

How much I must criticize you, my church, and yet how much I love you!
How you have made me suffer much and yet owe much to you.
I should like to see you destroyed and yet I need your presence.

You have given me much scandal and yet you alone have made me understand holiness.
Never in this world have I seen anything more obscurantist, more compromised, more false,
and yet never in this world have I touched anything more pure, more generous, and more beautiful.

Many times I have felt like slamming the door of my soul in your face – and yet how often I have prayed that I might die in your sure arms!

No, I cannot be free of you, for I am one with you, even though not completely you.

Then, too – where would I go? 'To build another church? But I cannot build another without the same defects, for they are my own defects I bear within me.

And again, if I build one, it will be my Church, and no longer Christ's.

No, I am old enough to know that I am no better than others.

I shall not leave this Church, founded on so frail a rock, because I should be founding another one on an even frailer rock: myself.

And then, what do rocks matter? What matters is Christ's promise, what matters is the cement that binds the rocks into one: the Holy Spirit.

The Holy Spirit alone can build the Church with stones as ill-hewn as we.

Carlo Carretto was an Italian monk who died in 1988. For many years he lived as a hermit in the Sahara Desert. He loved the church deeply, but he wasn't blind to its faults and failures, and he wasn't afraid to point out those shortcomings.

End.

Sean Walsh.

'**Has worked** in communications all his life – journalist, subeditor, editor, preacher, poet, dramatist, director, producer, former Head of Drama, RTE Radio… has steered many a creative writing workshop.
Loves words – how they sound, the challenge of getting them in the right order on page after blank page…

'Tells himself at the start of every writing stint: *when you've written something, lad, you haven't – you've written only the first draft...* (Rubbish, mostly!..)

'While cherishing the words of Maya Angelou: *The idea is to write it so that people hear it – and it slides through the brain and goes straight to the heart...*

And that in the only language he knows: Hiberno-English – English as it is spoken and written on the wee island of Ireland... 'May explain why he much prefers monologue, dialogue to narrative prose.

Few words. Simple. Lean meat. The ring of Truth. The music of assonance, alliteration. Melody. No sham, padding... Yes! Oh, yes!

'Took him years to arrive at the beginning of every writer's voyage: to be content in his own skin, write from within himself...

Sometimes in stooping down to pick up two pennies one can lose a fortune...

It doesn't just happen – you have to make it happen.
You make your way by taking it.

When you've written something, you haven't – you've written only the first draft...

Let the editing begin! Cut through the fat to get to the fillet... Delete, eliminate.
The lean meat will only be exposed by a merciless wielding of the scalpel.

His famous imitation of a Drama director!

His plays have been broadcast on RTE, BBC and – in translation - on European networks; televised on RTE, BBC One and Channel 4; staged at the Abbey National theatre (the Peacock, studio space), the Project Arts, the London fringe and the Liverpool Playhouse.

Credits include *The Dreamers, Earwig, The Search for Xavier, Assault on a Citadel, Centre Circle, Fugitive, Far Side of the Moon, Notes on the Past Imperfect, Veil, Pilate Under Pressure, The Night of the Rouser, 125 Valium Valley, Dead Man Talking, Travels with my Dad.*

A number of his scripts published on Amazon… paperback and Kindle. Also: Smashwords.com

Website: www.sean-walsh.me

Set against the backdrop of the first Good Friday

VEIL

"There is someone - something - in there but it is not our Misach..."

"Who are you? We are – the Cold..."

SEAN WALSH

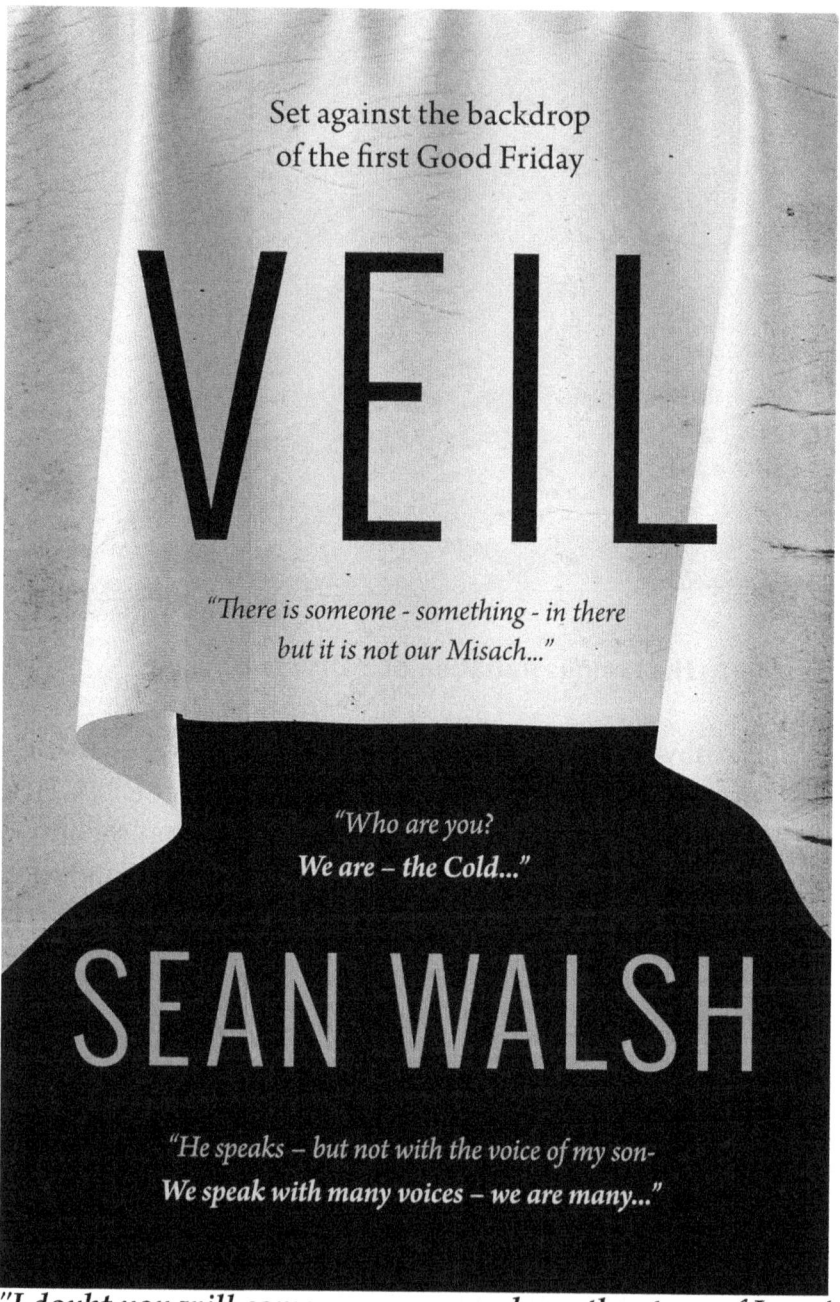

"He speaks – but not with the voice of my son – We speak with many voices – we are many..."

"I doubt you will come across an angle on the story of Jesus' passion and death which even remotely reflects what is to be found in this play. It is truly sui generis, one of a kind." - Martin Hogan

"His habit, Father – Xavier's habit
is hanging on the back of his door..."

THE SEARCH FOR XAVIER

SEAN WALSH

"If we attempt a cover-up we'll be denying Zavier… What?.. The prayers of the Faithful… the intercession of the people of God…"

This play shows why art is needed - to go where history cannot: in this case into the internal impact of a 'defection' from the fortress church of Irish Catholicism in the 1960s.

Xavier, a monk, has disappeared, but why - and what will this mean for the morale and mission of his brothers? How are they to make sense of it and what does the future hold for 'the church' anyway, a church over-identified then and now with its celibate clergy?

That question is not yet past history of course: 'The Search for Xavier' helps the reader - and not just the Irish Catholic reader - to articulate those questions we tend to suppress because of the 'Seamus Heaney Protocol': "whatever you say, say nothing".

It obviously took great courage for Sean Walsh to write this story, but it is also his skill as a writer that makes the book one of those as yet unknown classics that historians of the future will need if they are to map our recent past and present.

No other book has taken me so close to the inner turmoil caused to that fortress church of the 1960s by the answering of a vocation to a life that can nourish the heart as well as the soul.

- Sean O Conaill.

JENNY ONE

Just when I was beginning to get the hang of Jenny One, she disappeared. Enter Jenny Two... Oh, oh.

SEAN WALSH

TWO

Is there life after Jenny Two?.. Yes! Oh, yes!.. Welcome, Jenny Three!

THREE

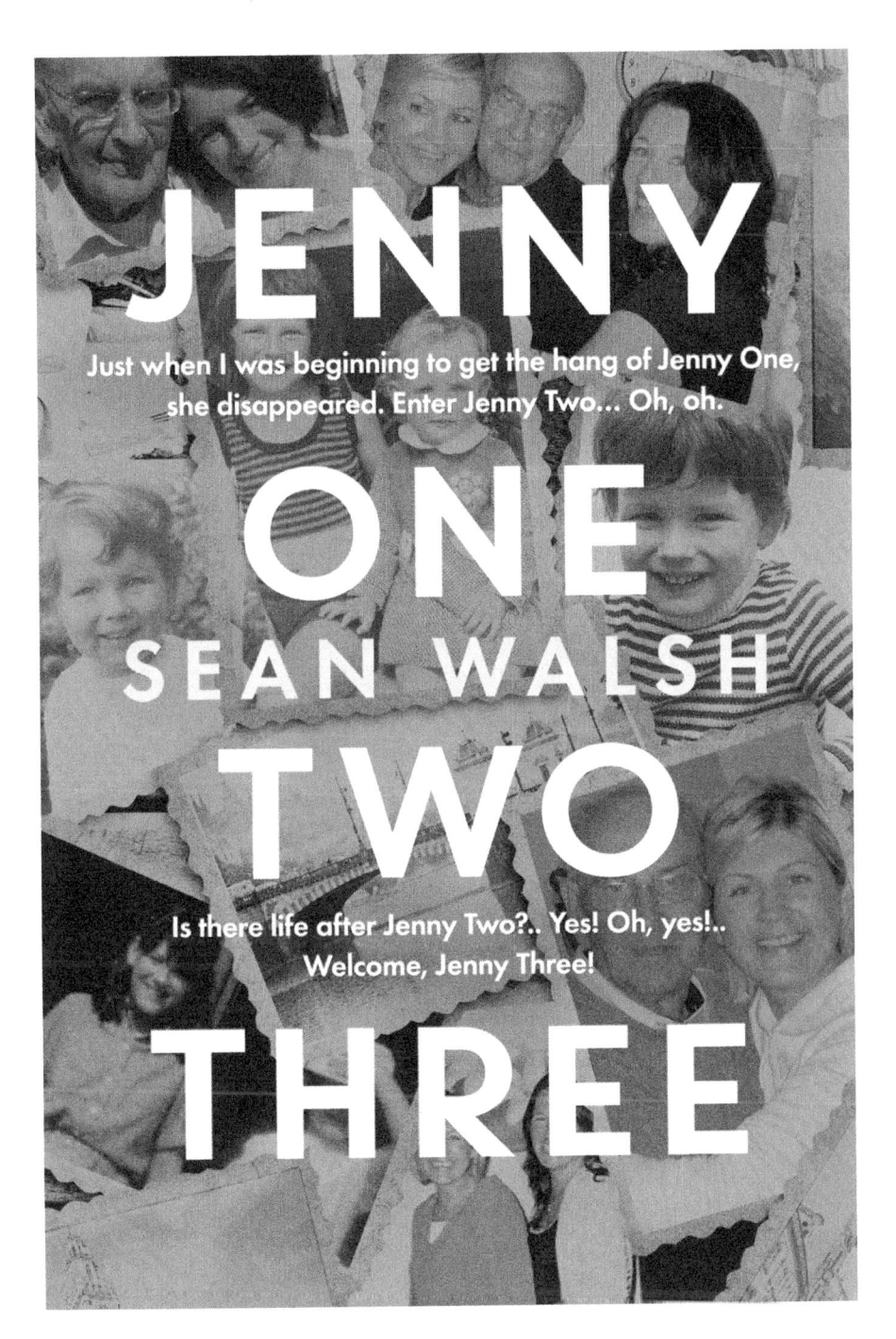

A love story – with a difference. A father's love for his two daughters, their love for their Dad.

TRAVELS WITH MY DAD

On the back, faded ink: Daddy, Rusty and Standard on the pier at Gyles Quay...

SEAN WALSH

Remember... Recall... Relive...
So long ago... seems like Yesterday.

"And Dad, Dad! Won't you take me with you again on one of your trips before not too much longer?!"

TRAVELS WITH MY DAD
SEAN WALSH

Rossnowlagh, Donegal.
"The Atlantic - I can wish!"

Nearing the end
of a long life I
look back...
in nostalgia.

ISBN 9798362950453

> *"I've had so many Tomorrows by now one more won't make much difference. And they're all the same as any Yesterday I've had for the past twenty years…"*

125 Valium Valley
Sean Walsh

"Baptised, the divil driven out of him, my first grandson… He'll live and die a Catholic now – though he might never know it…"

"It was a treat – and a great study of story-telling at its best…
'Something we see less and less of these days – a well structured play…

A first act of very funny exposures, told in the crispest, machine-gun dialogue… All six (members of the cast) reveal a dark time in our social history – explored and fought about in a sea of blind-folding alcohol and/valium.

Act Two. The various strings pulled together in an explosion of Baptismal farce that would reduce any audience to hysterics!..

But within, there is a seam of truth, of seriousness, of voices crying in the wilderness – and there is no missing this intention in the sobering Anew MacMaster monologue in the final moments of the play.

A laughter-filled but very dark, dramatic treat.

Bernard Farrell.

Never forget that writing is as close as we get to keeping a hold on the thousand and one things – childhood, certainties, cities, doubts, dreams, instants, phrases, parents, love – that go on slipping, like sand, through our fingers.
— Salman Rushdie

Made in the USA
Middletown, DE
16 February 2023

Made in the USA
Middletown, DE
16 February 2023